Daily Behavior Report Cards

The Guilford Practical Intervention in the Schools Series

Kenneth W. Merrell, Founding Editor
T. Chris Riley-Tillman, Series Editor

www.guilford.com/practical

This series presents the most reader-friendly resources available in key areas of evidence-based practice in school settings. Practitioners will find trustworthy guides on effective behavioral, mental health, and academic interventions, and assessment and measurement approaches. Covering all aspects of planning, implementing, and evaluating high-quality services for students, books in the series are carefully crafted for everyday utility. Features include ready-to-use reproducibles, lay-flat binding to facilitate photocopying, appealing visual elements, and an oversized format. Recent titles have companion Web pages where purchasers can download and print the reproducible materials.

RECENT VOLUMES

Response to Intervention, Second Edition: Principles and Strategies for Effective Practice
Rachel Brown-Chidsey and Mark W. Steege

Child and Adolescent Suicidal Behavior:
School-Based Prevention, Assessment, and Intervention
David N. Miller

Cognitive Therapy for Adolescents in School Settings
Torrey A. Creed, Jarrod Reisweber, and Aaron T. Beck

Motivational Interviewing for Effective Classroom Management: The Classroom Check-Up
Wendy M. Reinke, Keith C. Herman, and Randy Sprick

Positive Behavior Support in Secondary Schools: A Practical Guide
Ellie L. Young, Paul Caldarella, Michael J. Richardson, and K. Richard Young

Academic and Behavior Supports for At-Risk Students: Tier 2 Interventions
Melissa Stormont, Wendy M. Reinke, Keith C. Herman, and Erica S. Lembke

RTI Applications, Volume 1: Academic and Behavioral Interventions
Matthew K. Burns, T. Chris Riley-Tillman, and Amanda M. VanDerHeyden

Coaching Students with Executive Skills Deficits
Peg Dawson and Richard Guare

Enhancing Instructional Problem Solving:
An Efficient System for Assisting Struggling Learners
John C. Begeny, Ann C. Schulte, and Kent Johnson

Clinical Interviews for Children and Adolescents, Second Edition: Assessment to Intervention
Stephanie H. McConaughy

RTI Team Building: Effective Collaboration and Data-Based Decision Making
Kelly Broxterman and Angela J. Whalen

RTI Applications, Volume 2: Assessment, Analysis, and Decision Making
T. Chris Riley-Tillman, Matthew K. Burns, and Kimberly Gibbons

Daily Behavior Report Cards: An Evidence-Based System of Assessment and Intervention
Robert J. Volpe and Gregory A. Fabiano

Daily Behavior Report Cards

An Evidence-Based System of Assessment and Intervention

ROBERT J. VOLPE
GREGORY A. FABIANO

Foreword by William E. Pelham, Jr.

THE GUILFORD PRESS
New York   London

© 2013 The Guilford Press
A Division of Guilford Publications, Inc.
72 Spring Street, New York, NY 10012
www.guilford.com

Printed in the United States of America

This book is printed on acid-free paper.

Last digit is print number: 9   8   7   6   5   4   3   2   1

The authors have checked with sources believed to be reliable in their efforts to provide information that is complete and generally in accord with the standards of practice that are accepted at the time of publication. However, in view of the possibility of human error or changes in behavioral, mental health, or medical sciences, neither the authors, nor the editor and publisher, nor any other party who has been involved in the preparation or publication of this work warrants that the information contained herein is in every respect accurate or complete, and they are not responsible for any errors or omissions or the results obtained from the use of such information. Readers are encouraged to confirm the information contained in this book with other sources.

Library of Congress Cataloging-in-Publication Data

Volpe, Robert J., 1964– author.
   Daily behavior report cards : an evidence-based system of assessment and intervention / Robert J. Volpe and Gregory A. Fabiano.
       pages cm. — (The Guilford practical intervention in the schools series)
   Includes bibliographical references and index.
   ISBN 978-1-4625-0923-2 (pbk.)
   1. Behavior modification.   2. Behavioral assessment.   3. Rewards and punishments in education.   4. Report cards.   5. Home and school.   I. Fabiano, Gregory A., author.
II. Title.
   LB1060.2.V65 2013
   370.15′28—dc23
                                                                        2012043898

*We dedicate this book to our parents, spouses, and children
for their support and inspiration, and to the children,
educators, and families who have taught us so much
about the best way to work in schools.*

*We are indebted as well to numerous, esteemed researchers
who invented, developed, tested, and disseminated research
on daily report cards. Without their work, ours would not
have been possible. Specifically, we would like to thank
George J. DuPaul and William E. Pelham, Jr.,
for the countless examples of instruction and advice
as our graduate mentors, and for providing
the early opportunities for us to learn about
how to use daily report cards effectively in schools.*

About the Authors

Robert J. Volpe, PhD, is Associate Professor in the School Psychology Program in the Bouvé College of Health Sciences at Northeastern University in Boston. His research focuses on designing and evaluating academic and behavioral interventions for students with disruptive behavior disorders. He also is interested in behavioral assessment, particularly with regard to designing feasible systems for evaluating the effects of intervention. Dr. Volpe has authored or coauthored over 60 articles and book chapters, is on the editorial advisory boards of the *Journal of Attention Disorders* and the *Journal of School Psychology*, and is Associate Editor of *School Psychology Review*.

Gregory A. Fabiano, PhD, is Associate Professor in the Department of Counseling, School, and Educational Psychology at the University at Buffalo, The State University of New York. His research focuses on developing and evaluating effective assessments and interventions for children with attention-deficit/hyperactivity disorder as well as related disruptive behavior disorders. Dr. Fabiano has authored or coauthored over 50 articles and book chapters. His work has been funded by the Administration for Children and Families, the National Institutes of Health, and the U.S. Department of Education. In 2007 Dr. Fabiano was awarded a Presidential Early Career Award for Scientists and Engineers, the nation's highest honor for early-career investigators.

Foreword

In 1973 I was sufficiently lucky to be asked by Dan O'Leary to work with him and a small group of graduate students to investigate and document whether a school–home note—now widely known as a daily report card (DRC)—would be an effective tool to use for improving behavior and academic functioning in hyperactive children (O'Leary, Pelham, Rosenbaum, & Price, 1976). The idea for this intervention came from an earlier article by Jon Bailey and colleagues (Bailey, Wolf, & Phillips, 1970) about the well-known Achievement Place program for predelinquents at the University of Kansas. Both journal articles demonstrated that a system in which parents give children rewards contingent on daily notes from teachers about children's behavioral goal attainment in school was an effective means of improving the behavior of children that we now characterize as having externalizing or disruptive behavior problems, including children with attention-deficit/hyperactivity disorder (ADHD). Both articles also noted that the DRC is a means of getting parents and teachers to communicate with each other on a regular basis regarding a child's academic and behavioral progress in school—an outcome that is widely viewed as essential to enhancing supports for learning in school settings for children with disruptive behavior.

From these modest beginnings, a large literature was developed in the 1980s and 1990s documenting the utility and effectiveness of DRCs as stand-alone interventions or components of behavioral interventions for disruptive children in elementary school. Robert J. Volpe and Gregory A. Fabiano have nicely and briefly discussed the history of DRCs in the research literature and highlighted the various reasons why DRCs can be such a useful component of school-based interventions for disruptive children. Indeed, I suspect that a review of the components of behavioral interventions for ADHD would reveal that DRCs are the most commonly used component of comprehensive intervention in school settings (e.g., Fabiano et al., 2009b), even in those employed in the large collaborative studies of psychosocial interventions for ADHD (MTA Cooperative Group, 1999) and conduct problems (Conduct Problems Prevention Research Group, 1999) funded by the National Institutes of Health.

At the same time as DRCs are ubiquitously employed in studies in educational and clinical settings, there is wide variation in how broadly and how well they are used in authentic school settings. For example, I have seen teachers send kindergarten children with ADHD home with "daily report cards" in which no specific goals beyond "behavior" had been identified for the child. The evaluation provided for the child and parents was a circle drawn around one in a row of seven faces with expressions ranging from smiles to frowns, with no links to specific behaviors shown by the child. Parents were encouraged to provide a reward for the child on the weekend if he or she had "positive" DRCs for every day of the week. Professionals who are well trained in behavior analysis or school psychology will immediately recognize that a report that does not specify targeted behavior, nor provide a specific link to a criterion for earning a reward, yet at the end of a week rewards a 5-year-old child with ADHD for unspecified good behavior is an intervention that will have no beneficial effects. However, parents and many school personnel have not received formal training in the skills necessary to develop good classroom behavioral interventions, and inadequate DRCs are an all-too-often occurrence.

Thus, I welcome a comprehensive updating of the procedures—both formal and informal—that school practitioners can follow to learn and adopt this useful tool in their classroom work with children who have disruptive behavior and academic problems in the classroom. Drs. Volpe and Fabiano are distinguished researcher-clinicians with many years of academic and applied experience in this domain, and they have provided an excellent guide for using DRCs. They have drawn broadly from the DRC literature and integrated a number of concepts, procedures, and examples into a smoothly flowing, concise book. I believe that they have succeeded in their goal of providing a user-friendly guide for school practitioners, as well as for graduate students and teacher trainees.

Although both brief and lengthy versions of "how to do a DRC" exist (e.g., my own online guide and Mary Lou Kelley's [1990] book, both cited in the Additional Resources section), this book steers a middle course. It provides a greatly expanded version of my 10-page form for teachers and parents, but it is not as lengthy as other comparable texts, which typically have numerous citations and explanations of contingencies and schedules of reinforcement. This book is written in language that school practitioners and teacher trainees without extensive experience in behavior modification will understand without difficulty, and it provides guidelines for and explanations and examples of all stages of DRC child screening, development, implementation, problem solving, and evaluation. A particularly relevant touch is the authors' attempt to link the DRC to the three tiers of intervention included in response-to-intervention and positive-behavioral-support paradigms, including a procedure for screening in regular educational classrooms. The authors demonstrate how the DRC can be used as a preventive Tier 2 intervention and a component of a Tier 3 intervention for a more seriously impaired child. In addition, they have highlighted the potential utility of a DRC as an idiographic progress monitoring tool, which I believe is one of its most useful aspects (Pelham, Fabiano, & Massetti, 2005).

I would like to close with a plea for more widespread use of psychosocial, as opposed to pharmacological, treatments for children with disruptive behavior in school settings. A DRC is a cost-effective intervention for children with school-based behavior problems that should be much more widely used. Currently, 9.5% of schoolchildren in the United States are diagnosed as having ADHD and two-thirds of those diagnosed are taking a prescribed stimulant medication for treatment focused primarily on the school setting. Despite many studies documenting that behavioral interventions are as effective as medication in controlling ADHD in classroom settings (Brown et al., 2008), medication continues to be a first-line treatment for children with ADHD and, increasingly, for related behavior problems. This trend persists despite the fact that medication has not been shown to be either safe or effective for long-term use in children with ADHD (e.g., Volkow & Swanson, 2008). Books such as this one can be effective in teaching school professionals that there are nonpharmacological approaches to ADHD that can go a long way toward providing safe and effective first-line treatment (Brown et al., 2008).

WILLIAM E. PELHAM, JR., PhD
Center for Children and Families
Florida International University

Contents

CHAPTER 1

Introduction

Disruptive student behavior in the classroom has long been a source of stress for teachers. Results of a 2004 survey found that over a third of teachers had seriously considered leaving the teaching profession or knew someone who had left because of difficulty handling student behavior problems. This issue was particularly evident for new teachers, with over three quarters of them feeling unprepared to deal with student behavior problems (Public Agenda, 2004). In another survey 25% of teachers ranked classroom management as their highest priority for professional development (Coalition for Psychology in the Schools and Education, 2006). In the same survey teachers also ranked highly the need to learn more about communicating with parents about the classroom behavior problems exhibited by their children. Most teachers get into the field because they want to support student learning. Yet, effective management of challenging behaviors is necessary in order to create an environment conducive to effective teaching.

PURPOSE OF THIS BOOK

This book is intended for those practitioners who are involved in supporting students with academic and behavior problems in school settings. This includes school-based practitioners, such as school psychologists, teachers, school counselors, guidance counselors, and principals, in addition to practitioners based outside of the school, such as clinical psychologists, behavior analysts, behavioral pediatricians, and social workers. This book is also intended for use by graduate training programs that prepare students to embark on the careers mentioned above.

The purpose of this book is to prepare you, the reader, to employ the daily report card (DRC) as a flexible and dynamic tool for promoting student behaviors that enable a student's success in school and, in so doing, diminish behaviors that get in the way of that success and the success of others. This is a translational book. Our goal is not to provide an exhaustive review of the literature on DRCs or to provide a purely academic discussion concerning DRCs. We are also not going to describe an intervention that we ourselves created. The DRC has been around as a school-based intervention for challenging classroom behavior for at least 40 years, and there are a number of resources that we would recommend for additional reading (see pp. 119–120 for an annotated bibliography and other resources). Rather, based on the available literature and our own experience in research and practice, we hope to provide you with the tools necessary to successfully implement DRC interventions in your own setting. Our key goals in this book are to provide you with an understanding of the strengths and limitations of the DRC as an intervention and measurement tool. Our intention is to provide you with a user-friendly guide to (1) identify students who would benefit from the DRC intervention, and (2) design and implement the DRC as an intervention or possibly use it solely as a measurement tool for progress monitoring. We also have provided a number of resources that will facilitate your use of the DRC and to maximize the benefits derived from your efforts. We do this because the DRC can be used in different ways with different students and across classrooms.

In the following sections of this chapter we describe the DRC and why you should be interested in using it as an intervention and assessment tool. Schools are increasingly moving toward tiered models of intervention that integrate problem solving, intervention, and monitoring into a systematic approach to support students who engage in challenging behaviors. Therefore we also discuss how the DRC fits into a three-tiered model of schoolwide prevention and intervention.

The following case example is based on our experience in working with children and youth in the school setting. We refer to this case example throughout the book to help the reader contextualize the concepts and procedures we discuss.

> Sky is an 8-year-old girl in a general education third-grade classroom situated in a small suburb. Sky has been earning A's and B's in school since first grade, but from the beginning of the current academic year, she has been falling behind her peers in math and her grades have suffered in several subjects. Sky's homework often is missing or incomplete, and she frequently does not complete her classwork in the time allotted. Sky's teacher, Mr. Bartlet, regularly reprimands her for talking to her peers in class, for humming loudly, and for walking around the room when she should be working. She tends to be "sassy" and often requires several reminders in order to follow directions. Mr. Bartlet is concerned about Sky's behaviors because they are disruptive to the other students in class, and he admits to being frustrated because his attempts to address these problems have not been successful.
>
> Sky's parents are concerned about the downturn in her grades and her diminished motivation for school. They have withheld television viewing and other privileges when they have heard bad news from Mr. Bartlet via e-mail or in quarterly reports, but they also admit to being somewhat inconsistent in their enforcement. Sky also reports that she "doesn't care" when they punish her, which has left her parents wondering whether they are doing the right thing. They regularly work with Sky on her homework and talk with her about how things are going at school (e.g., when tests and projects are due, how she is behaving). However, what they hear from Sky seems to be inconsistent with reports from her teacher, as she often indicates to her parents that things are going well at school.

The case of Sky is fairly typical of the types of problems we see in our work in schools. A common story that we hear from the parents with whom we work is that they often are surprised when reviewing their child's quarterly report cards. Grades that fall below parental expectations often are punctuated by comments such as "not working to potential," "frequently distracted," "chatty," or "talks back." Parents tell us, with exasperation, that they ask their child everyday how things are going in school and the answer is almost always the same: "Good." We often hear about brief spurts of improvement following quarterly report cards, but such gains are typically short-lived. For many children, quarterly report cards of academic performance and school behaviors are an effective means of monitoring progress and managing contingencies, and they continue to be used across grade levels. For other children, however, it is clear that more frequent feedback and coordination between the school and home setting regarding school performance are necessary.

WHAT IS THE DRC?

The tools and procedures we discuss in this book fall under an umbrella of strategies that affords a systematic method for providing frequent (e.g., one or more times daily) feedback to students on their behavior. Since such interventions first appeared in the research literature in the late 1960s, these tools have been known by many names in addition to DRC including "daily behavior report cards" (Schumaker, Hovell, & Sherman, 1977) or "daily report cards" (O'Leary & Pelham, 1978), "home-based reinforcement" (Bailey, Wolf, & Phillips, 1970), "home notes" (Blechman, Taylor, & Schrader, 1981), and "home–school notes" (Kelley, 1990). The overwhelming majority of studies has focused on providing intervention to individual students. However, there are examples in the literature of classwide administration, and often more than one student in a classroom has received the intervention simultaneously. A host of different formats and procedures, all based upon the same underlying principles, has been used successfully to address a wide array of academic and disruptive classroom behaviors. We discuss several different formats of DRC in Chapter 4; here we would like to give you a general idea of the types of DRC we focus upon in this book.

When we refer to the *DRC*, we are talking about all of the materials and procedures that are used in the process of implementation. A key tool in the implementation of the DRC is the DRC form. Figure 1.1 is an example of a DRC for Sky. A DRC form consists of a clearly defined list of behaviors that have been deemed appropriate targets for intervention (e.g., interrupting, noncompliance, academic productivity, academic engagement). Associated with each item is a means of rating the target behavior (usually in terms of frequency, duration, or percentage complete) across one or more observation intervals (e.g., time of day or class period). In some cases, the goal for each behavior is included in the wording of the item (e.g., *fewer than eight instances of inappropriate noises*, as in the first item of our sample DRC for Sky), and teachers rate each item using a "yes" (goal was met) or "no" (goal was not met) format. In other cases the teacher can rate the frequency of the item or rate the item on a scale and then record whether a predetermined goal was or was not met. As part of the DRC procedures teachers provide regular feedback to the child regarding target behaviors, as well as liberal praise for working toward and/or meeting daily goals. DRC forms are sent home with the child each day, and parents review daily and weekly progress and provide home-based privileges (e.g., use of bicycle, computer time) contingent on meeting goals. Thus, the home and school are linked on a daily basis—a critical component for children when consistency and coordination across settings are essential (Dussault, 1996; Koegel & Koegel, 1996). In addition, a DRC provides a record of

	Reading	Writing	Math	Science
Fewer than eight instances of inappropriate noises.	Y N	Y N	N/A	N/A
Starts work with fewer than two reminders.	Y N	Y N	Y N	Y N
Completes assignments within allotted time.	Y N	Y N	Y N	Y N
Talks back fewer than two times.	Y N	Y N	Y N	Y N

Date: 2/29/2012

Completed _____% of assigned homework.   Number of Yeses _____   Number of Nos _____

Mr. Barlet's Comments: _____

_____

_____

Home Rewards and Comments: _____

_____

_____

Mr. Barlet's Initials: _____   Parent's Initials: _____

FIGURE 1.1. Example of a DRC for Sky.

student progress over the course of intervention. When used as an intervention, there are three basic components to the DRC: (1) the rating of the DRC form, (2) frequent encouraging teacher feedback regarding progress toward goals, and (3) home-based rewards and encouragement for reaching goals. As mentioned earlier, a DRC also can be used as a measurement tool to assess student response to an intervention other than the DRC (Riley-Tillman, Chafouleas, & Briesch, 2007). We further discuss the use of the DRC as a measurement tool in Chapter 7.

HOW DO DRCs WORK?

There are two main ways by which the DRC is thought to enhance the behavior and academic outcomes of children. First, for many students for whom the use of the DRC is warranted, school has become a frustrating environment, where most of the feedback they receive from teachers is negative (e.g., corrective or reprimanding). Such an approach places emphasis on negative behavior, and in some cases can increase problem behaviors by rewarding them with teacher attention. Moreover, conflict between children with behavior problems and their teachers is a strong predictor of later problems (Hamre & Pianta, 2001; Ladd & Burgess, 2001). Studies have found rates of teacher praise to be particularly low for students with behavior problems (e.g., Shores et al., 1993; Wehby, Symons, & Shores, 1995). Increasing teacher praise has been demonstrated to improve reading outcomes (Gable & Shores, 1980), to increase academic engagement (Sutherland, Wehby, & Copeland, 2000), and to decrease disruptive behavior (Gunter, Denny, Jack, Shores, & Nelson, 1993).

In contrast, the DRC approach advocated in this book is a positive one, wherein only desired behaviors are attended to, encouraged, and rewarded. The items on DRC forms can be positively worded and teachers told to provide positive and encouraging feedback throughout the day as students work toward achieving their daily goals. This focus on positive behaviors and goal attainment should also result in a classroom environment with a better balance between positive and negative feedback. This balance is important; teachers and parents should strive to achieve the "magic ratio" of 5:1 positive to negative interactions with children because higher ratios of positive to negative interactions have been found to predict favorable attitudes toward work and relationships and are a component of an effective approach to classroom management (Fabiano et al., 2007). Moreover, there is evidence that children who have more supportive exchanges with teachers are better liked by their peers (see Hughes, Cavell, & Wilson, 2001).

Second, most children with significant behavior problems will require some contingency management approach and parental involvement for meaningful school improvement to be achieved (Pelham & Fabiano, 2008). The school–home communication and home-based contingencies (i.e., rewards/privileges for appropriate behavior) may each contribute to the effectiveness of the DRC and also nurture child investment in meeting daily goals or goals established for smaller increments of time (e.g., one class period that may be problematic for the student). By placing a child in an earning situation at the start of each school day (e.g., "If I meet my goals, I can participate in fun after-school activities"), children are placed in a position to succeed and make good choices. This is different from the all-too-common approach of taking away privileges after failing to meet goals (punishments that often are ambiguous, reactive, and unexpected—in these cases the child is unsuccessful and it is too late for him or her to make a good choice. Together, these consequences of DRC implementation can work to foster improved classroom behavior and academic functioning.

WHY SHOULD I USE DRCs?

In addition to the DRC's positive approach to intervention, there are several other advantages that make it an attractive option for promoting behaviors that are related to success in school settings. In this section we discuss the evidence base for DRC use, its efficiency and acceptability, its flexibility, and its utility in linking systems in support of students.

Several decades of research support the efficacy of the DRC. One of the first published reports of using the DRC can be traced back to work in the 1960s when middle school students with significant behavior problems in a residential program attended a special summer classroom at the University of Kansas (Bailey et al., 1970). As an example of the behavior problems, in the academic year prior to the study one boy had missed so much academic instruction because of time spent in the principal's office that he ended up having to repeat the grade. Initially, while the students attended the summer class, they received no DRCs. Later in the study, students were sent home with a positive note each school day, regardless of their behavior in class. Under this condition, the children showed no improvement. The children also did not improve when the teacher provided specific feedback on whether each child met established behavioral goals. It was only after the specific feedback was linked to rewards in the home that the children improved in their behavior. In fact, once the specific feedback was linked to these home consequences, all the children improved and began behaving appropriately in the classroom almost 100% of the time. Given the seriousness of the behaviors exhibited by children at the beginning of the study, these results were quite remarkable. They also teach us an important lesson: Feedback, warnings, and good news notes alone may be insufficient for some students, and feedback should be linked to positive consequences in the school or home setting.

Following this early study, many more investigations have demonstrated that a DRC is an effective way to improve functioning of children in both regular education and special education settings. Moreover, several studies have supported the use of DRC as a best practice for improving the classroom performance and behavior of students with attention-deficit/hyperactivity disorder (ADHD) in general education (O'Leary, Pelham, Rosenbaum, & Price, 1976) and special education (Fabiano et al., 2010). Indeed, the Department of Education lists the DRC as a cornerstone intervention for students with ADHD (U.S. Department of Education, 2004).

The DRC can be an unobtrusive and efficient intervention strategy. Since ratings can be completed in less than 1 minute, alterations to teacher classroom practice are minimal (Lahey et al., 1977). The DRC is also an efficient and effective procedure for monitoring outcomes in important areas of children's psychosocial functioning (Pelham, Fabiano, & Massetti, 2005; Riley-Tillman et al., 2007). The DRC has been found sensitive both to pharmacological (e.g., Pelham et al., 2001) and behavioral treatment effects (e.g., Pelham, Massetti, et al., 2005).

The efficiency of the DRC is an important consideration because the time needed to implement an intervention is a key factor associated with how acceptable it is to teachers (Witt, Martens, & Elliott, 1984). One of the reasons acceptability is important is because it is thought to be an important determinant in the degree to which teachers use an intervention at all and whether they implement the procedures consistently. Witt and Elliott (1985) proposed a theoretical model of acceptability that hypothesizes a reciprocal relationship between the acceptability of a treatment, its use, the degree to which it is implemented as prescribed, and its effectiveness. Few studies have actually investigated the degree to which teachers find the DRC an acceptable intervention approach. Chafouleas, Riley-Tillman, and Sassu (2006) conducted a survey of teachers concerning their use and acceptance of the DRC. A total of 64% of the 123 teachers who returned surveys reported using some kind of DRC. The study makes clear that teachers use the DRC for a variety of purposes (a communication tool, an intervention to change behavior, a tool to monitor behavior) and that they use an assortment of different approaches to DRC-related interventions with respect to who receives the intervention (e.g., individual student, whole class), types of consequences provided (verbal, tangible) and where the consequences are delivered (school or home). Overall, the teachers surveyed reported that the DRC was an acceptable approach for both assessment and intervention. Very little information is available as to how parents and children perceive the DRC. Only one study by Lahey et al. (1977) provided encouraging results in this regard. The acceptability of the intervention among teachers and parents likely supports its use. Another factor that would seem to support the consistent use of the intervention is that teachers and parents use the procedures each school day. An approach such as the DRC explicitly addresses potential teacher drift and maintains, on a daily basis, the teacher's attention to behavioral goals. This aspect of the DRC encourages consistency because the procedures quickly become routine. Also, teachers and parents create permanent products recording their adherence to many of the procedures. That is, teachers record their ratings on the form, and parents sign the forms to acknowledge their receipt and to record when rewards are dispensed. One advantage of continuously monitoring child behavior is that important changes are documented in real time so that the DRC can sound an alarm. If there is a day or two when the child is not meeting goals, this report should alert parents and teachers that something is amiss and they need to problem-solve regarding the intervention or possibly other areas of functioning.

Teacher feedback to the child regarding progress toward goals may also serve as an antecedent to future appropriate behavior by the child (Sugai & Colvin, 1997) and contribute to amenable parent–teacher relationships (Dussault, 1996). Thus, in addition to acute beneficial behavioral effects, the DRC may also be a helpful enhancement to the important relationships between parents, teachers, and children (Pianta, Steinberg, & Rollins, 1995) as well as serve as a data-driven monitoring device with which schools can evaluate the progress of children demonstrating academic and behavior problems. Information collected via the DRC provides outstanding feedback for annual reviews of progress toward individualized education plan (IEP) goals and empirically informs adjustments to the IEP (e.g., Fabiano et al., 2010; Vannest, Burke, Payne, Davis, & Soars, 2011). Indeed, the DRC can help increase communication and collaboration between home and school, which is mandated by special education law (e.g., Public Law 94-142), and the DRC is a practical mechanism through which these requirements can be realized.

Finally, the DRC procedure may be an essential enhancement to IEP programming by preventing teacher drift from engaging in the practices designed to meet the explicit goals and objectives operationalized in the IEP. It is now well established that a single to a few consultation visits are insufficient to maintain significant change in teachers' approach to students with behavior/learning problems (Fuchs & Fuchs 1989; Martens & Ardoin, 2002), and teachers and other school staff often require explicit instruction and guidance in the process of establishing a behavioral intervention plan (e.g., Horner, Sugai, Todd, & Lewis-Palmer, 2000).

BRIEF OVERVIEW OF THIS BOOK

We believe it is important to contextualize the DRC in a three-tiered model of problem solving. Schools across the country are implementing schoolwide plans to support positive social behavior and academic achievement. Typically initiatives for academics and social behavior have been implemented independently, but recently there have been increasing calls for an integrated approach (McIntosh, Goodman, & Bohanon, 2010; McKinney, Bartholomew, & Gray, 2010). This call for integration makes sense because the links between academic and behavior problems are well established. In addition, the same conceptual model (see Figure 1.2) applies well across academic and behavioral domains. In each tier of the model students receive supports (whether in an academic or behavioral domain) that are commensurate with their individual needs. Each student's level of need is determined by data gathered at each tier.

In Tier 1 (universal instruction and supports) all students receive research-based instruction with special focus on universal behavioral interventions or the instructional areas known to impact student improvement. School professionals are familiar with the five big ideas in reading (i.e., phonemic awareness, alphabetic principle, fluency, vocabulary, and comprehension) delineated by the National Reading Panel. In terms of behavior, schools typically generate three

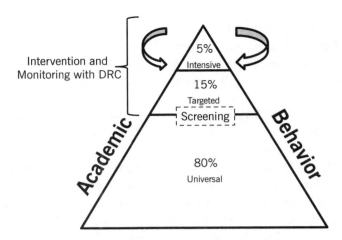

FIGURE 1.2. The three-tiered problem-solving model.

to five expectations that reflect social competence (e.g., be there, be ready, be responsible, be respectful). These expectations are made explicit, and students receive regular encouragement to meet them. In Tier 1 all students are screened several times over the course of the school year to inform school staff about the effectiveness of instruction in Tier 1 and to identify students who are not responding adequately to that instruction. In Tier 2 (targeted intervention and supports) students receive intervention in the identified problem area in addition to the instruction provided in Tier 1. In Tier 2 students are assessed more frequently to monitor their response to interventions and to facilitate decision making for troubleshooting the Tier 2 intervention or determining whether more intensive supports are necessary. It is expected that most students will respond to the supports provided in Tier 1 and Tier 2, but approximately 5% of students will need more intensive intervention. In Tier 3 (intensive interventions) assessment and intervention efforts become more idiosyncratic and may exceed the resource demands that are afforded in the general education setting. In Tier 3 student response to intervention should be assessed regularly, and interventions should be designed based on individualized assessments. In the behavioral domain such assessments typically involve functional behavioral assessment.

This book is designed to provide tools for use at each of the three tiers in the aforementioned problem-solving model. We have developed a model for screening and intervention based on the DRC. In Chapter 2 we provide an overview of the model we call the Integrated Screening and Intervention System (ISIS; Volpe, Fabiano, & Briesch, 2012) and explain how the model can be used to conduct universal screening in Tier 1 to identify students who might benefit from DRCs. We believe that DRCs are an excellent choice for a Tier 2 intervention (see Vannest et al., in press) and can serve as a foundational component of a Tier 3 intervention package. DRCs support both the academic and behavioral sides of the problem-solving model. Although they do not target academic skills directly, they traditionally have targeted both academic productivity and engagement/motivation, which are considered key behaviors that enable academic success (e.g., DiPerna, Volpe, & Elliott, 2001, 2005; Volpe et al., 2006).

In Chapters 3 and 4 we provide detailed information concerning the construction of DRCs and the procedures that are necessary for successful implementation. In these chapters we explain how the ISIS can be used to streamline the process of DRC design and implementation. In Chapters 5 and 6 we discuss important considerations and provide tools for working with students and parents, respectively. Chapter 7 is dedicated to considerations for using the DRC as a progress monitoring tool. This chapter discusses measurement concerns and also provides a framework for making decisions based on data gathered using a DRC.

Chapter 8 (authored by Amy M. Briesch and Brian Daniels) explores the process of transitioning from a DRC intervention to a self-management intervention for the purpose of maintaining the gains of the DRC intervention and promoting self-regulation and generalization to settings not targeted directly in the DRC intervention. To paraphrase the beloved Scottish poet Robert Burns, our best-laid plans often go askew, and so we have dedicated Chapter 9 solely to the topic of problem solving a DRC-based intervention. This chapter discusses common pitfalls we have experienced in our use of DRCs and suggests recommendations on how to refine the DRC forms and procedures to maximize the impact of the intervention.

This book contains an extensive set of documents to help facilitate your use of DRCs. Throughout the book we refer to forms that we have provided to streamline the process of implementing the DRC. In addition, we have made available several digital forms for charting DRC data. These are available for purchasers to download at *www.guilford.com/volpe-forms*.

CHAPTER 2

Identifying Students
Who Might Benefit from a DRC

Tiered models of prevention increasingly have become a major stimulus for discussion and action in schools. A critical element in such models is to identify students who are not benefiting from universal instruction so that they may receive additional supports in order to prevent or reduce more serious problems. Consensus continues to grow around the notion of proactively identifying and treating children at risk as an alternative to the wait-to-fail model (see Glover & Albers, 2007). In the academic realm we now have curriculum-based measurement probes and benchmark standards to help school professionals determine which students are at risk for academic failure in core areas of the curriculum, and these measurement tools have strong treatment validity. By *treatment validity* we mean that data generated from these measures are useful in identifying areas of concern, informing intervention planning, and in evaluating intervention outcomes (see Gresham, 2005). The number of elementary schools conducting schoolwide screenings for academic risk (particularly in the area of reading) has dramatically increased over the past decade.

Unfortunately, for several reasons including the stigma associated with labels for mental health problems (see Kauffman, Mock, & Simpson, 2007), very few schools conduct schoolwide screening assessments for emotional and behavior problems (Romer & McIntosh, 2005). Focusing solely on academic skills is unfortunate, because the relationship between emotional and behavior problems has been well established and likely is reciprocal (e.g., Hinshaw, 1992).

A wide array of screening instruments and procedures designed to identify students demonstrating emotional and behavior problems now is available. Lane, Menzies, Oakes, and Kalberg (2012) have provided an excellent resource to assist schools in selecting screening procedures to meet their individual needs. Included in this resource is a detailed review of six schoolwide screening systems and a useful framework for selecting the appropriate system based on several factors, including school demographics, constructs of interest, available informants, time, and monetary considerations. Common approaches to screening in the emotional and behavioral domains include office disciplinary referrals (ODRs; McIntosh, Frank, & Spaulding, 2010), multiple-gated screening procedures (e.g., Severson, Walker, Hope-Dolittle, Kratochwill, & Gresham, 2007), and brief rating scales (e.g., Kamphaus, DiStefano, Dowdy, Eklund, & Dunn, 2010). One common limitation to these screening approaches is that they are somewhat limited in terms of treatment validity. Typically screening and assessment for treatment planning (e.g., functional behavioral assessment) are distinctly separate tasks (see Cook, Volpe, & Livanis, 2010). One exception would be the Social Skills Improvement System (SSIS; Elliott & Gresham, 2007), which includes both screening (the SSIS Performance Screening Guide) and intervention materials (SSIS Classwide Intervention Program, SSIS Intervention Guide).

Another exception would be ODRs, which typically are used both for screening and for progress monitoring. Unfortunately, using ODRs as an assessment is limited in that they are sensitive only to a narrow set of behaviors that would result in disciplinary action, which typically are only the most severe behavior problems that can occur in school (e.g., physical aggression). As such, they are not sensitive to a wide array of behaviors that impact classroom functioning and student learning, but do not result in referrals to the principal's or disciplinarian's office. These concerns are not trivial, as in our experience, schools are reluctant to screen students for problems when they feel unprepared to deal with the issues that may be revealed. This stance leads to a reactive approach to addressing behavior problems wherein teachers refer students to a child study team (at best) or for a psychoeducational evaluation when serious problems emerge. Typically these referrals occur only after behavior problems have become more difficult to manage and bad habits may be more entrenched for both the student and teacher.

Before discussing screening in more depth, it is important to acknowledge that for some children, no formal screening procedure is necessary. A kindergartener who frequently runs out of the classroom, bites peers, and does not acknowledge adult requests to stop, clearly requires immediate and intensive intervention. For most students, however, behaviors will not be as pronounced as those in this example, and teachers may find a classwide screening to be a helpful approach for separating typically developing students from those who require additional supports. With the advent of tiered models of intervention, in which schools carefully consider who needs what, for how long, and at which level of intensity, screening approaches are the means of doing so.

In this chapter we provide an overview of the Integrated Screening and Intervention System (ISIS; Volpe et al., 2012), which we designed to address many of the problems associated with existing screening approaches and to streamline the process of implementing DRC procedures. The ISIS can be used to assist classroom teachers in the process of nominating students for intervention, or it can be used for students who already have been identified as at risk via one of the aforementioned screening procedures (e.g., SSBD). We have not yet begun

---

SOME COMMERCIALLY AVAILABLE UNIVERSAL SCREENING MEASURES

Systematic Screening for Behavior Disorders (Walker & Severson, 1990)
www.soprislearning.com

BASC-2 Behavioral and Emotional Screening System (Kamphaus & Reynolds, 2007)
www.pearsonassessments.com

Social Skills Improvement System: Performance Screening Guide (Elliott & Gresham, 2007)
www.pearsonassessments.com

Student Internalizing and Externalizing Behavior Screeners (Cook, Gresham, & Volpe, 2012)
www.psiwaresolutions.com

to evaluate the technical characteristics of the ISIS screening procedure, but have used it to assist teachers in nominating students in need of DRC interventions and to develop individual DRCs in several classrooms. Several studies have demonstrated the validity of teacher nomination procedures for identifying students with externalizing behavior problems (Caldarella, Young, Richardson, Young, & Young, 2008; Lane, Wehby, Robertson, & Rogers, 2007; Kalberg, Lane, Driscoll, & Wehby, 2011; Ollendick, Greene, Weist, & Oswald, 1990). Furthermore, we believe that the ISIS procedures can be used to streamline the process of consulting with individual teachers when implementing a DRC. However, in the absence of technical data, the ISIS screening procedure might best be viewed as a second step of the screening process, wherein an empirically supported procedure is used first to identify risk status, and the ISIS screening procedure is used as a second step to assess the degree to which the DRC is a suitable intervention and to streamline the DRC design process.

In describing the ISIS below, we assume that either a DRC has been chosen as a Tier 2 intervention as part of a schoolwide initiative, or if working with an individual teacher, that a DRC has been deemed an acceptable intervention for that teacher (considerations with regard to student acceptability are discussed in detail in Chapter 5). If the acceptability for any intervention is low, it is unlikely to be delivered with integrity, if at all, and efforts to positively impact student behavior will suffer.

THE ISIS

The ISIS (Figure 2.1) is a model that links the process of screening to the design of DRC interventions. In this book we describe the ISIS and provide you with a series of tools to facilitate your use of the model. We have drawn heavily from Bergan (1977) and Kratochwill and Bergan (1990) in creating the ISIS. Bergan's behavioral consultative problem-solving model consists of the following four stages: (1) problem identification, (2) problem analysis, (3) implementation, and (4) problem evaluation. To avoid confusion, it is important to note that we have

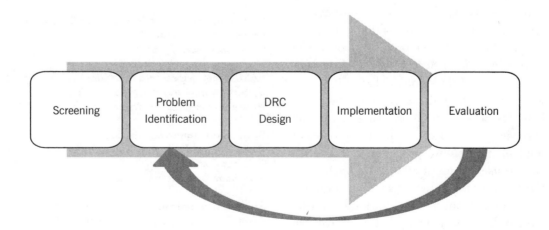

FIGURE 2.1. The ISIS model.

used Bergan's model only as a general framework for conducting the interviews necessary for implementing the DRC. The Bergan model was structured around developing hypotheses and designing interventions with regard to the function of problem behaviors; however, there is no explicit consideration of functional relationships in the ISIS model. Also, the ISIS was designed expressly for the purpose of streamlining the process of designing and delivering DRC interventions.

We believe that there is sufficient evidence in the research literature to support the use of a DRC as a Tier 2 intervention for children who exhibit disruptive classroom behavior. The intervention is effective, efficient, and sufficiently flexible to address a wide array of common problem behaviors; it links and focuses home and school supports; and it generates data that are useful in evaluating effectiveness. We have found that providing a discrete structure to the tasks involved in screening, designing, and implementing DRCs enhances the degree to which the process is manageable and efficient. Given all the time constraints placed on school professionals, manageability and efficiency are important considerations. Functional analysis is more likely to occur in Tier 3, given the time and levels of expertise involved. Although we do not discuss functional assessment in this book, the processes of problem identification and data collection that are part of the ISIS model can be used to facilitate functional assessment for students who do not demonstrate an adequate response to DRC intervention. Clearly, the processes of problem identification, data collection, and intervention components such as adult attention, access to preferred activities, and the like, involve functional thinking. That is, through monitoring student behaviors in response to manipulations in these variables, we gain valuable insights into functional relationships between problematic behaviors and the child's environment.

Figure 2.1 indicates the five stages of the ISIS: (1) screening, (2) problem identification, (3) DRC design, (4) implementation, and (5) evaluation. In this chapter we provide a detailed description of the screening stage of the model by describing the steps involved in identifying students in a classroom who would most benefit from the DRC. Later steps in the process are addressed in more detail in subsequent chapters.

Using the ISIS, a consultant can implement a sound DRC intervention efficiently through a set of brief interviews and brief check-in contacts with a classroom teacher and one or more parents/guardians. We discuss four types of interviews in this book that should be led by the consultant: (1) the Screening Interview, (2) the Problem Identification Interview, (3) the DRC Design Interview, and (4) the DRC Evaluation Interview.

The first interview, the Screening Interview, should involve a school-based team (as in the case of schoolwide screening) or a teacher (in the case of classwide screening), where the objective is to create a prioritized list of students who might benefit from a DRC intervention. The Problem Identification Interview should be conducted with the classroom teacher and the student's parent(s). Although more than one student might be identified in the screening process, because of the sensitivity of the information to be discussed, the teacher should meet with each student's parent(s) separately. The objectives of the Problem Identification Interview are to (1) establish a list of problem behaviors, (2) arrange for the collection of baseline data, and (3) plan for the next steps of the process.

The objectives of the DRC Design Interview are to create the DRC form (including the goals for each item) and identify the procedures for implementation and evaluation of the DRC intervention. In the DRC Evaluation Interview progress monitoring data are reviewed. The objectives are to (1) determine the extent to which the goals of the intervention have been met, (2) assess the acceptability of the intervention, and (3) decide what changes to the intervention plan, if any, are necessary.

SCREENING

The ISIS Teacher Rating Form (ITRF) can be completed by teachers prior to an initial interview (Figure 2.2; Appendix A). This measure was designed to serve the dual purpose of identifying and rank-ordering students who might benefit from DRC intervention and to link teacher-reported problem behaviors directly to DRC items targeting those specific behaviors. The ITRF can be completed for students already identified via an empirically supported screening method (e.g., ODR, SSBD). Teachers might also complete the form for any additional students about whom they may be concerned. It is certainly possible that students not meeting a criterion on a broadband screening measure might still benefit from a DRC, and indeed that such students might develop more severe problems overtime if early problems are not addressed. Also, if by some other means it is determined that a particular student would benefit from a DRC, the screening interview can by skipped and the teacher can complete the ITRF prior to the Problem Identification Interview.

Items of the ITRF were derived from high-frequency DRC items and target behaviors from a study evaluating a DRC intervention for a group of 63 children with ADHD (Fabiano

Teacher: _____ School: _____						
Date: _____ Grade: _____						
Directions: This form can be used to rate student behavior that interferes with their learning or the learning of others. In the long columns on the right, please list the names of the five students in your classroom whose behavior is of greatest concern to you in this regard. For each item below indicate your level of concern regarding each student using the following scale: **1 = Slight concern** **2 = Moderate concern** **3 = Strong concern** Leave the space blank if the student does not exhibit the behavior or if the behavior is not a concern for that student.	Student Name	Student Name	Student Name	Student Name	Student Name	
1. Does not complete classwork on time						
2. Inaccurate or incomplete classwork						
3. Does not start assignments independently						

FIGURE 2.2. The ISIS Teacher Rating Form (Volpe, Fabiano, & Briesch, 2012).

et al., 2010). We sought to identify items for the ITRF that could easily be linked back to DRC items to streamline the design of DRC forms. Items on both the ITRF and DRC were further refined by pilot work we conducted in elementary schools in the Boston Metro area. Directions for the ITRF ask teachers to identify five students in their classroom whose behavior "interferes with their learning or the learning of others." Space on the form allows teachers to record the name of each of these five students. This is somewhat similar to the multiple-gated screening procedure of the SSBD (Walker & Severson, 1990), wherein teachers first rank students and then complete ratings only for students with the highest rankings. The initial step or gate of the procedure dramatically reduces the number of students a teacher needs to rate, and so significantly reduces the time required to complete the screening process.

Once teachers have identified the students to be rated, they read each item on the ITRF and rate the behavior of all of the students identified in the first step. We have organized the form to allow teachers to rate all five students at the same time. There are 43 problem behaviors to be rated on the form and two blank items that teachers can use to fill in problem behaviors not captured elsewhere on the rating form. Some behaviors of concern can be quite idiosyncratic, so we have left these items blank to afford flexibility and to keep the number of items to a manageable level. Each item on the ITRF is worded as a problem behavior (e.g., "Does not complete classwork on time," "Argues with teacher," "Does not work well with others"). Teachers are instructed to leave blank items that are not of concern to them and to rate those that do cause them concern with a value from 1 to 3 (slight concern = 1, moderate concern = 2, strong concern = 3).

The ITRF is scored by summing the item ratings for each student for a Total Problems score. The Total Problems score provides an estimate of the level of concern for each student, and can be used to create a rank-ordered list of students who would benefit from a DRC. Also, ratings for each problem item can be used to help prioritize behaviors to target for treatment for one or more students. Although teachers may be experiencing significant concerns for more than one student, we find that many teachers are reluctant to initiate individual interventions with more than one student at a time, particularly when the teachers are unfamiliar with the intervention procedures. Generating a rank-ordered list helps establish priorities in addressing each student's difficulties. That is, once the teacher is accustomed to intervening with one student, it is relatively easy to move down the list to the remaining students.

Screening Interview

The Screening Interview Form (Appendix B) can be used to structure the Screening Interview with teachers or a child study team. The Screening Interview Form is organized around four key tasks of the Screening Interview with the objective of establishing a prioritized list of students who might benefit from a DRC intervention. Prior to the interview the ITRF should be scored and student names and their Total

SCREENING INTERVIEW TASKS

1. **Examine rankings from ITRF and make adjustments based on the magnitude of teacher concern.**

2. **Assess the fit of the DRC for each student.**

3. **Organize follow-up tasks.**

4. **Establish prioritized list of students.**

5. **Schedule Problem Identification Interview.**

Problems scores should be entered into the Student Ranking Table, which is provided on the Screening Interview Form (see Figure 2.3). List the student with the highest Total Problems score in the first row (rank 1) and continue the process until all of the rated students' names and scores are recorded on the form.

In the example shown in Figure 2.3, the teacher has provided ratings for five students, with Sky (described in Chapter 1) having the highest Total Problems score (TP = 44) and Giorgio having the lowest (TP = 6). At the Screening Interview, the first task is to establish whether the teacher agrees with the ranking of students. That is, do scores on the ITRF correspond with the rank order of teacher concerns with regard to rated students? We have found that, in general, scores derived from the ITRF are consistent with teacher priorities for intervention—particularly for the top-ranked students—but certain behaviors represent a greater concern than others, and it makes sense to use rankings from the ITRF as a point of departure for decisions regarding ranking rather than relying on them exclusively.

The second task in the Screening Interview is to assess the fit of a DRC intervention for each of the students who has been ranked. The ITRF was designed to identify students whose problem behaviors are a good match for the intervention, but several issues may raise questions as to whether a DRC is an appropriate intervention for a given student. The most obvious issue pertains to the student's parents. If the parents are known to use harsh disciplinary practices or if significant problems with communication with parents are expected, the DRC likely is a poor fit unless it is modified for school-based as opposed to home-based reinforcement. Likewise, if the student's behavior problems are judged to be too severe or if significant internalizing problems are of primary concern, other intervention approaches should be considered. The "Fit" column of the Student Ranking Table can be used to indicate these concerns. We have listed some common abbreviations on the form to note concerns with regard to fit (AA = additional assessment, FP = follow-up with parent, SBR = school-based reinforcement, IP = internalizing problems are a primary concern).

Because these discussions can generate several follow-up tasks, the third task in the interview is to establish a plan to address these tasks. The table on the second page of the Screening Interview Form can be used to record follow-up tasks for those students (e.g., pursue other intervention solutions, arrange for additional assessment, follow up with parents). Each follow-up task should be recorded clearly in this section along with information indicating who will perform the follow-up action and when this should be accomplished.

Rank	Total Rating	Student	Fit	Priority
1	44	Sky	✓	1
2	32	Brian	FP	2
3	28	Max	✓	3
4	20	Jim	✓	3
5	6	Giorgio	✓	N/A

FIGURE 2.3. Student ranking from the Screening Interview Form.

Once potential fit issues have been discussed, you can proceed to the next step of the interview, which is to determine the priority for each student for which the DRC is thought to be appropriate. Use the "Priority" column to note the priority of the remaining students, based on each student's Total Problem score and the teacher's preference. In some cases, information gathered through the follow-up procedures may warrant a reordering of priority rankings. In our example, Sky clearly should be the highest priority student for a DRC. She has the highest problem score and the fit was considered to be good. However, the problem scores for Brian and Max are similar. The teacher has had far less contact with Brian's parents and is unsure whether the home-based reinforcement component of the intervention is feasible. Some follow-up with parents is necessary to estimate the fit of the intervention in this regard. The priority ranking of Brian and Max may require adjustment after the teacher talks with Brian's parents.

The final step of the Screening Interview is to schedule a time for the Problem Identification Interview. The procedures for this interview are the focus of Chapter 3.

Problem Identification

In the previous chapter we discussed the process of identifying students in need of intervention, which involved administering the ITRF and conducting the Screening Interview. Through this process a prioritized list of students was created starting with the student with the most significant concerns. We also mentioned that in some instances the student in need of intervention already has been identified, and in such cases the ITRF can be used to aid in the design of a DRC by identifying potential DRC items and prioritizing them by the level of teacher concern. After screening students or, in the case of working with single students, scoring the ITRF, the next step in the process is to conduct a Problem Identification Interview.

In this chapter we outline the procedures for the Problem Identification Interview and for the collection of baseline data. Since the process of problem identification involves operationally defining and measuring target behaviors, we discuss these issues in detail. It is beneficial to have one or more parents or guardians involved in each step of the process moving forward. Chapter 6 addresses the topic of working with parents, and we have included the DRC contract and a sample parent letter in Appendix G that explains the DRC process to parents. We recommend contacting the parent by phone before sending this letter. Parents cannot always attend the meetings discussed in this book for several reasons, but that need not inhibit the process.

THE PROBLEM IDENTIFICATION INTERVIEW

Once one or more students have been selected for intervention, the Problem Identification Interview can be conducted with the teacher and one or more parents. The objectives of the Problem Identification Interview are as follows: (1) select and rank-order potential targets for intervention, using scores generated by the ITRF and discussion with the teacher; (2) operationally define these behaviors; and (3) establish procedures for baseline data collection. The Problem Identification Interview Form (PIIF; Appendix C) can be used to prepare for the interview and to create a record of the meeting. We have kept this form as lean as possible because, in our experience, interviews with parents and teachers typically are brief, and there are many demands competing for the consultant's attention. We have made these forms available for purchasers to download as word processing files at *www.guilford.com/volpe-forms* so that they can be easily modified to suit your specific needs.

SELECTING POTENTIAL TARGET BEHAVIORS

On the first page of the PIIF is a table that can be used to record the behaviors of greatest concern to the teacher and parent. Figure 3.1 contains an example of a completed table for our case study of Sky. Concern ratings for each ITRF item can be used to help choose four to six problem behaviors as potential targets for intervention. Our goal in the DRC design process is to create a DRC form that includes between three to five items, but if time permits, it is helpful to identify additional behaviors at this stage of the process. These additional behaviors of concern can be targeted once the student consistently meets the goals linked with the initial pool of behaviors. The first column of the table can be used to prioritize potential target behaviors. A "1" should be entered next to the highest-priority target behavior, a "2" for the next highest-priority item, and so on.

> **PROBLEM IDENTIFICATION INTERVIEW TASKS**
>
> 1. **Select and rank-order target behaviors.**
> 2. **Operationally define each target behavior.**
> 3. **Establish procedures for baseline data collection.**
> 4. **Plan for next steps.**
> 5. **Schedule DRC Design Interview.**

Behaviors Targeted by the DRC

A number of target behaviors are appropriate for inclusion on DRC forms. Table 3.1 lists the most common behavioral and academic targets that were included on a DRC in a yearlong study. In this study, IEP for children with ADHD in special education were reviewed with teachers, and the goals/objectives listed on the plans were transformed into targets that could be evaluated throughout the day by the child's teacher. During this task, it was clear that goals generally fell into one of two broad categories: academic behavior or social behavior. Within categories, a few goals occurred very often, and others were used sparingly or for individual cases. For example, in the social domain, about a third of children had a target related to following directions. In contrast, one child had a target to refrain from "bargaining." This particular child

Ranking	Problem Behaviors	DRC Item
1	Disrupts others	Makes *X* or fewer inappropriate noises
		Fewer than *X* instances of talking when not appropriate
2	Does not start assignments independently	Starts work with fewer than *X* reminders
3	Does not complete classwork on time	Completes assignments within the allotted time
4	Argues with teacher	Talks back fewer than *X* times
5	Missing or incomplete homework	Completed *X*% of assigned homework

FIGURE 3.1. Selection of potential target behaviors table for Sky.

TABLE 3.1. List of Daily Report Card Targets and the Percent of Children with Each Target

Academic target	Percent	Social target	Percent
Returns completed homework[a]	100	Follows directions with X or fewer reminders	33
Stays on task with X or fewer reminders	40	Respectful to teacher/Accepts feedback appropriately	32
Completes assignments in specified amount of time	28	X or fewer instances of negative behavior toward peers	23
Completes assignments with X% accuracy	18	Raises hand with X or fewer reminders	17
Begins work with X or fewer reminders	17	Remains in assigned seat or area with X or fewer reminders	17
Organized/Prepared/On-time for class	17	When upset, will display appropriate coping behaviors	15
Answers/Responds to teacher questions	12	Keeps hands/feet to self with X or fewer reminders	13
Writing goal (Writes X sentences/Uses Correct spelling/Writes legibly	10	Works quietly/interrupts with X or fewer reminders	8
Completes Work with X or fewer prompts reminders	10	Appropriate behavior in specials/cafeteria	8
Begins work independently/No more than X requests for help	10	Has X or fewer class rule violations	7
Specific target for reading class	7	Has X or fewer outbursts/tantrums	5
Uses time appropriately after completing assignments	5	Breaks pencil X or fewer times	2
Returns to task after prompt with X or fewer reminders	5	Follows transition rules appropriately	2
Completes assignment in math class	3	Has X or fewer instances of "silly" behavior	2
No more than X instances of moving ahead in the lesson	3	Makes appropriate eye contact with others	2
Homework completed at home with X% accuracy	3	No more than X instances of bargaining	2
Completes morning routine according to checklist	3		
Records homework in planner appropriately	3		
Turns in assignment appropriately	2		
Checks over work before handing it in	2		

Note. X = the criterion set for each child based on teacher consultation.

[a]Targeted for all children in the study as part of study methods.

From Fabiano et al. (2010). Copyright 2010 by the National Association of School Psychologists. Bethesda, MD. Reprinted with permission of the publisher; *www.nasponline.org*.

often debated or attempted to negotiate with adult demands, and this was a behavior that was irritating to the teacher and resulted in class disruption. As this example illustrates, the DRC can target behaviors that occur at high rates in classrooms, as well as behaviors that may occur less frequently across students.

It is worth noting that educators may also choose to define a class of behaviors more broadly to capture a whole class of behaviors in a single item. Take academic productivity, for example. Many teachers will want a child to complete an assignment within a given time at a rate of accuracy that demonstrates understanding and application of class content. Many targets may address this behavior, such as "Stays on task"; "Completes assignment in time given"; "Completes assignment accurately"; and "Begins work without multiple prompts." Even a target such as "Stays in assigned seat or area" may be related to academic productivity, and therefore targeting work completion may address the out-of-seat behavior as well, if it is primarily a work-avoidant behavior. In other words, if a student is working hard to earn a reward based on work completion and accuracy, he or she may remain seated while working to reach the criterion even if it does not relate explicitly to remaining seated. Given all these choices, a first guideline would be to choose or craft a target that captures the problem behavior in the simplest manner possible; complicated targets are harder for teachers to evaluate and for children to remember and understand. Thus, "Completes all work with at least 80% accuracy within the time given" may be a single target that addresses multiple areas of impaired functioning (e.g., remaining on task, starting work on time, remaining seated).

On the last two pages of the PIIF (Appendix C) we have provided the "DRC Item Table" (see Figure 3.2 for some sample items), which links screening items from the ITRF to high-frequency DRC items. In many cases, several DRC items are associated with individual items on the ITRF. For example, there are five potential DRC items associated with item 15 on the ITRF ("Disrupts others"). We chose to design the ITRF this way to minimize the length of the measure, and in turn, minimize the time required for teachers to complete it. The DRC Item Table can be used to link teacher concerns to specific DRC items and to begin the process of developing operational definitions for each target behavior (we discuss this process in more detail below). Potential DRC items can be recorded in the third column, as displayed in Figure 3.1 for Sky.

Figure 3.1 presents an example wherein the teacher is interested in targeting two of Sky's behaviors associated with the "Disrupts others" screening item. Notice in this table that many of these items are incomplete. For example, the first item—"Makes X or fewer inappropriate noises"—requires a definition of "inappropriate noises" and the value of X. It is important to determine what exactly the teacher means by "inappropriate noises" and to establish how often this behavior occurs. We take a data-based approach to establishing these values for X, but first the behaviors must be operationally defined. Once the items for the DRC are established, teachers will rate each item as "Yes" (the goal was met) or "No" (the goal was not met). Some items can be rated once a day (e.g., "Brings completed homework to class"), but most of the items will be rated several times throughout the day (e.g., by class period or activity). Although we favor the dichotomized rating approach because of its inherent simplicity, there are other common methods of rating DRC items (discussed in detail in Chapter 4). Also, we cannot foresee every possible scenario, so you may need to create some items from scratch. The list of items that appear in the DRC Item Table in Figure 3.2 can be used as models in the creation of new items. Keep in mind that it is important that items should reflect student behaviors that are readily observable.

Screening Items	DRC Items
Does not complete classwork on time	• Completes assignments within the allotted time • Stays on task with *X* or fewer reminders
Inaccurate or incomplete classwork	• Completes *X* assignments with *Y*% accuracy • Completes *X*% of assigned work
Does not start assignments independently	• Starts work with *X* or fewer reminders
Argues with teacher	• Talks back fewer than *X* times
Missing or incomplete homework	• Brings completed homework to class • Completes *X*% of assigned homework • Writes homework in assignment book with *X* or fewer reminders
Does not turn in class assignments	• Turns in assignments appropriately
Does not correct own work	• Corrects assignments appropriately

FIGURE 3.2. The DRC Item Table for Sky.

OPERATIONALLY DEFINING TARGET BEHAVIORS

Before collecting baseline data, we must first establish operational definitions for each of the target behaviors that have been identified. Operational definitions are formal ways of establishing what constitutes an occurrence of the behavior of interest. It provides a way of translating one person's subjective concept of a student's behavior into objective and observable terms so that it can be measured reliably by other people. Three considerations for writing good operational definitions are that a definition should be (1) objective (i.e., it should describe observable characteristics of the behavior and minimize reliance on inferences made by the observer), (2) clear (i.e., the definition should be free of jargon and unambiguous), and (3) complete (i.e., the boundaries of the behavior should be established; Hawkins & Dobes, 1977, as cited in Kratochwill & Bergan, 1990). If you have done a good job writing an operational definition, a person who does not know the student could identify the behavior based solely on the operational definition.

A good operational definition is . . .

1. **Objective** (i.e., it should describe observable characteristics of the behavior and minimize reliance on inferences made by the observer).
2. **Clear** (i.e., the definition should be free of jargon and unambiguous).
3. **Complete** (i.e., the boundaries of the behavior should be established).

If you examine the partial list of DRC items in Figure 3.2, you will see that some items require little clarification. For example, the DRC item "Completes assignments within the allotted time" would not appear particularly controversial, particularly if the assignment was to complete all the problems on a math worksheet. However, the next item, "Stays on task with *X* or fewer reminders," requires consideration as to what constitutes *on task* and what constitutes a *reminder*. Many other items contain the word "appropriately", for example, "Turns in assignments appropriately." Here the definition of what is *appropriate* will differ from one classroom to the next, so it is important to define what is meant by *appropriate* as it relates to these behaviors in the setting of interest. For example, asking for help appropriately could be operationally defined as "Raises hand to ask for help without disturbing other students (e.g., by making loud noises or kicking desk)."

Once operational definitions have been articulated for each of the target behaviors, the next step is to establish procedures for data collection. Three factors that need to be determined prior to data collection are (1) the person responsible for data collection, (2) what will be recorded and how, and (3) when data should be recorded.

ESTABLISHING PROCEDURES FOR BASELINE DATA COLLECTION

It is important that the collection of baseline data begin immediately so that intervention is not delayed. The teacher is the logical person to be responsible for data collection. Since the DRC intervention requires the teacher to keep track of target behaviors, it makes sense for the teacher to take on this role. The consultant should be responsible for creating materials that will facilitate the collection of baseline data, and to check in with the teacher to ensure that procedures are being conducted as planned. In the Problem Identification Interview, procedures are established for collecting these data.

In our practice we often are confronted with resistance to the collection of baseline data. It is not surprising that teachers who have been struggling with problem behavior enough to seek help would show some resistance to delaying intervention. They want the problem fixed *now*. The collection of baseline data, however, is an essential component of DRC procedures for several reasons. First, baseline data establish the typical level and variability in the behaviors in which we are interested. By comparing baseline data to expected levels of behavior, we can establish the presence or absence of a problem. By *problem* we mean that there is a gap between a student's current and expected level of performance. Second, baseline data inform the selection of goals for the DRC intervention. We could set the goal for each DRC item at the level of behavior we wish to see exhibited by the child, but in most cases incremental short-term goals are necessary for the student to be able to earn rewards and benefit from the intervention. Third, baseline data establish a point of departure from which to evaluate the effectiveness of the DRC. Although our initial inclination may be to dive right in and start with the intervention, it is important to demonstrate to all stakeholders that the intervention is working. Just as important, baseline comparisons allow us to know when the intervention is not working, which enables us to modify ineffective procedures or to otherwise troubleshoot the intervention. Trying to make a decision as to the effectiveness of an intervention without baseline data is like trying to navigate with a compass when you don't know where you are. The degrees on a compass are meaningful only if we have some idea of where we are and where we want to go. We know this as data-based decision makers, but perhaps a more convincing argument for teachers is that the baseline data collection procedures actually are the first step in training the teacher to carry out the intervention. Being able to keep track of student behavior is a core element of the intervention, and collecting these data across the target behaviors in each setting of interest is a critical element in the DRC design process.

Charted baseline data should be reviewed at the next interview (the DRC Design Interview). In some cases, baseline data may already be available by way of existing permanent products. Examples include inaccurate or incomplete homework or classwork assignments, not correcting or checking work, and writing illegibly. The teacher's grade book or collection of completed work assignments can be reviewed to establish a level of baseline responding. Some form of observation will be required, however, for other target behaviors.

Several additional elements of data collection require clarification before the collection of baseline data can begin. First, the dimension of measurement of the target behaviors must be established. This is a simple task for the majority of items included in the DRC Item Table.

Dimensions of Measurement

Baseline data for almost all of the items in the DRC Item Table can be obtained using event recording to measure frequency of occurrence. Such recording is useful when the behaviors of interest have a discrete beginning and end, as one can simply keep track of the number of times the behavior occurs during an interval.

In some cases the behavior is dependent on another event that may occur several times during an interval. For example, one of the items selected for Sky is "Starts work with fewer than X reminders." Some students have difficulty beginning work only during a particular class and so only one episode need be recorded. However, in other cases students have difficulty initiating work several times throughout a class. In such cases it is necessary to record several frequencies. For example, in the case of Sky, she may start one worksheet with only one reminder but may have needed five reminders to begin another task during the same class. Then again, she may have started one task with no reminders, then stopped working and needed several reminders to resume work. For items such as this, the frequency of each episode (beginning/ resumption of work) should be recorded. Later both the average number of reminders (e.g., three) as well as the range of frequencies can be examined. In this example we are interested not only in the student's behavior, but also the teacher's behavior. Also, since we are measuring teacher behavior (i.e., reminders), we would like to be able to compare the values of reminders across occasions. As such, we want to standardize the delivery of reminders. An example of a standard reminder procedure would be as follows:

1. Teacher makes the request.
2. If no compliance after 10 seconds, teacher repeats request verbatim.
3. Teacher repeats step 2, if needed.

In some cases we are interested in whether the behavior was exhibited or not in an interval, such as a class period (e.g., "Uses materials appropriately," "Keeps hands and feet to self"). Such items can be recorded with Yeses and Nos. Although one could use a check or slash to indicate a "Yes," with the absence of a mark representing a "No," this system is not recommended because it is difficult to know for sure whether a blank box represents a "No" or instead represents an item that was not recorded. Other items involve obtaining a proportion of behavior. For example, the item "Complies with $X\%$ of teacher demands" would require noting both the number of teacher demands and the number of times the student complied with those demands. For such items it is important to specify in the operational definition how much time is allotted to the student to comply with a demand. For example, "Record noncompliance when the student does not comply with a teacher demand within 15 seconds." This item can be modified to allow for a reminder. A procedure could be added using something similar to the standard reminder procedure provided above. That is, noncompliance could be recorded if the student did not comply after such a reminder. One method of keeping track of demands and compliance is to use a vertical line "|" to record a demand and to add a horizontal line to it "+" if compliance occurs.

When it is important to know how long a behavior lasts or how long it takes to complete a task, the unit of interest is duration (e.g., "Returns from water fountain or bathroom within X minutes"). Recording for this item would involve a stopwatch or some other device and a procedure to record either elapsed time or the time it was when the student left the room and when he or she returned. Duration is often the unit of interest when dealing with tantrums. In other cases you may be interested in the time between some event and the onset of a specific behavior. For example, you may be interested in the latency between a teacher's request (e.g., "Take out your textbook") and student compliance. Data collection might also require a timing device, unless the teacher is free to undertake a silent count, which might be feasible when latencies are relatively short (< 10 seconds).

Observation Intervals

In establishing procedures for baseline data collection it is advantageous to break up the day into intervals that are salient to the teacher who is serving as the data collector. Typically, intervals coincide with subject areas or class periods, although some behaviors can be recorded one time per day (e.g., "Has all needed materials for homework in backpack at the end of the day," "Completed $X\%$ of assigned homework"). If transition times are an area of concern, these should be included as additional intervals (e.g., time on the bus, school arrival, hallway or classroom transitions). Also, if the teacher reports that there are specific periods of the day when the behaviors of interest are not a concern, eliminating these settings or times from data collection can streamline the process.

In Appendix D we have provided the Baseline Data Collection Form, which can be used to record operational definitions for target behaviors and the baseline data itself. The form is suitable for recording the frequency of up to six target behaviors for five intervals over 5 days. The form may prove cumbersome for recording multiple durations or proportions, so please access and modify the online form to suit your purposes. Once the procedures for baseline data have been established, they should be carefully explained to the teacher, with time allowed to address any elements that may not be clear. It is best to have the teacher repeat back the procedures to ensure that both the teacher and consultant are in agreement on how to proceed.

PLANNING FOR THE NEXT STEPS

One of the last tasks of the Problem Identification Interview is to schedule a check-in with the teacher. The purpose of the check-in is to ensure that procedures for baseline data collection are being followed correctly and to answer any questions that might have arisen. The ideal time for an initial check-in is at the end of the first day of data collection. If data collection has not gone smoothly on the first day, the procedures can always be modified or clarified without losing too much momentum. It is always a good idea to check in one or two times more over the baseline period, just to encourage the teacher to keep the process moving forward. In addition to scheduling this check-in, it is a good idea to let the teacher and parent know how best to contact you, should questions arise. The last step in the Problem Identification Interview is to schedule a time for the next meeting (the DRC Design Interview). If the parent is not present, arranging a time when he or she might be able to attend this next meeting may require some follow-up.

The process of collecting baseline data may be new to the teacher and will likely require some adjustments to well-established routines. Sometimes such data collection goes very smoothly. When data collection does not go smoothly—and by that we mean when data are not recorded—it can be easy to feel discouraged and at this point consultants often question the commitment of the teacher to engage in the intervention process. For various reasons, some teachers are better able to engage in the process than others. If this is the first time a teacher has engaged in this type of activity, it may be challenging, and certainly teachers working with children with behavior problems have many forces and pressures competing for their attention. As much as the process of baseline data collection is useful for establishing an estimate of what is typical behavior for the target student, it also is a field trial for how a teacher can manage monitoring the behaviors of interest. Since this is an essential element of DRC, it is wise to use the week of data collection to pare down or simplify the process if necessary.

It is acceptable to shorten the list of target behaviors to ease the data collection for teachers, as this will translate to a simplification of the DRC form itself. One factor to consider is how broadly defined the behaviors are. We use the example of the work completion item, "Completes $X\%$ of assigned work with $Y\%$ accuracy." This item, in most cases, can be used as a good broad indicator that the student is academically engaged. Of course we have seen situations when the student completed all of his or her work ahead of other students and then becomes disruptive, and in such cases other items may be more appropriate and additional considerations may come to mind. Another feature of the work completion item also is worth noting. This item, like several others in the DRC Item Table, does not require the teacher to observe behavior during instruction. As we mentioned earlier in the chapter, some items can be measured through a review of permanent products (e.g., homework, completed in-class assignments).

CHARTING BASELINE DATA

One of the tasks the consultant will need to complete before the DRC Design Interview is to chart baseline data and make a determination as to whether the data are adequate to proceed. As we noted earlier, the collection of baseline data serves several purposes, including clarifying the presence of a problem, informing goal setting, and forming a point of departure by which to evaluate the effectiveness of the DRC intervention (cf. Cooper, Heron, & Heward, 2007). In order for baseline data to satisfy these purposes, it is necessary to aggregate and summarize them in such a way as to facilitate accurate decision making.

Before baseline data can be charted, the method of aggregation first must be determined. Using the baseline data collection plan for Sky as an example, the fictional teacher (Mr. Bartlet) collected data on the following six target behaviors: (1) frequency of inappropriate noises, (2) frequency of talking when inappropriate, (3) number of teacher reminders before Sky begins assignments, (4) completes assignments in the allotted time, (5) frequency of talking back, and

(6) percent of homework completed. Based on the teacher's report, these behaviors were of concern in four classes (reading, writing, math, and science), so these classes served as intervals for data collection. Figure 3.3 summarizes data for the first item (frequency of inappropriate noises) by charting the frequency (the y, or vertical, axis) of the target behavior by class period (as represented by the four data series) across 5 school days (as indicated by the intervals on the x, or horizontal, axis).

Figure 3.3 was created in Microsoft Excel. We often use Excel to store and graph data because we find that the graphing and data storage capabilities are adequate for our purposes. Some people prefer to use an online program such as ChartDog, which can be found at *www.interventioncentral.com*, for graphing. Indeed, some holdouts still use paper and pencil, which offers convenience, but arguably makes it more cumbersome to manipulate and share data. Each person knows what works best for him or her. Working in black and white for the purposes of this book, we have used empty and filled shapes and dashed and solid lines to make it easier to distinguish the four data series, each of which represents an interval (class period), although the use of color can more readily differentiate each data series. To remind us of the specific behavior of interest, we include the operational definition of the target behavior beneath the chart.

In many ways these are good baseline data, but we will withhold our discussion on that topic for the next chapter. Here our discussion is related to how best to summarize data. We can see that if we simply averaged the data for each day across class periods, the observed frequency of Sky's noisemaking would range between five and six or so times per day. Although the data are very stable from day to day, in aggregating data this way we would lose important information concerning the differences in Sky's inappropriate noise making across class periods. If the frequency were more comparable across class periods, it might be acceptable to aggregate (sum) the data by day to simplify the presentation of data (i.e., one data series compared to four).

This method of charting frequencies would be appropriate for half of Sky's target behaviors (also appropriate for "frequency of talking when inappropriate" and "frequency of talking back") and the overwhelming majority of items on the DRC Item Table. The same type of chart

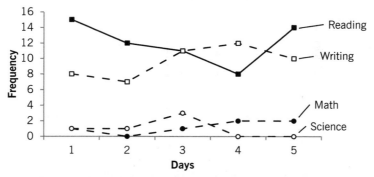

Inappropriate noises are noises that are distracting to others, including sound effects, humming, singing, or shouting of any kind.

FIGURE 3.3. Baseline data for inappropriate noises by class period.

can be used also to summarize percentages, as in the item for percentage of homework completed. The only difference would be the label of the *y* axis (*percentage* instead of *frequency*), and the values would typically range from 0 to 100%.

The third item for Sky—the one relating to the number of reminders before she begins an assignment—is slightly different, because Sky may have several assignments to do in a single interval. One way to summarize the data would be simply to chart the average number of reminders needed in each class period. A chart of those data might look very much like Figure 3.3. This might be appropriate if the range of reminders was relatively narrow (although with the appropriate operational definition and perhaps a different range of values on the horizontal axis). If there is quite a bit of variance in the data, it may be more useful to chart that variability as in Figure 3.4. This information can be very useful for goal setting. These data also were charted in Excel by using the High–Low–Close chart type option, which typically (we assume) is used for charting stock values. For our purposes, we entered the highest number of reminders in the High column, the lowest number in the Low column and entered the average number of reminders in the Close column. The only disadvantage is that this approach allows you to plot only one data series at a time.

Charting frequency and proportion data can be relatively straightforward and clearly summarizes baseline data, but charting yes–no or binary data may not be much of an improvement over the raw data itself. For example, let's say that we are interested in tracking the item "Uses materials appropriately." Based on the data collection plan, the teacher has rated this item once each class period across four different classes (math, science, social studies, and music). Since there only are two possible values for each assessment (e.g., day 1 math), if we charted a time series as in Figure 3.3, it would be difficult to interpret. That is, if the data were presented in a bar graph, there would be columns reaching up to the maximum value (i.e., 1) and then there would be an absence of bars for nos (0's). A line graph would not represent much of an improvement, because the lines might cross one another often as the charted values fluctuated between

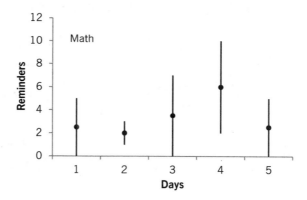

Reminders = The number of times that Sky is reminded to begin work using the phrase "Sky, get to work" before she begins to do her work (e.g., starts completing a math problem, starts to read an assignment).

FIGURE 3.4. Baseline data for reminders for math.

the two values of 1 and 0. One way to address this issue is to aggregate the data by summing the yeses for each class over the 5 days of data collection, as in Figure 3.5.

This is a good way to take a first look at the data because it indicates potential differences across intervals. In this case the student always used materials appropriately in social studies and often used materials inappropriately in math, science, and music (perhaps because these classes utilize many materials). So, the top panel of Figure 3.5 could prove very useful for deciding where to target this behavior. Unfortunately, the chart is not particularly useful for establishing a point of departure for measuring the effectiveness of the DRC intervention. However, if we sum the frequency of yeses across classes for each day, we can obtain a time series of the overall frequency of the target behavior, as in the bottom panel of Figure 3.5. Here we set the maximum value on the y axis to be the maximum number of yeses that could possibly have been

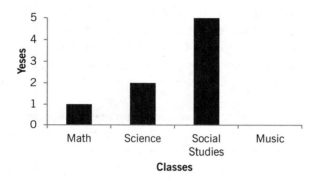

Uses materials appropriately is coded "yes" when the student uses materials for their intended purpose (e.g., writing with a pen, measuring with a ruler or using it as a straight edge) or if the student does not use materials inappropriately. Code "no" if the student uses any object inappropriately during an interval (e.g., disassembles a pen, makes a paper airplane, bends paperclips out of shape)

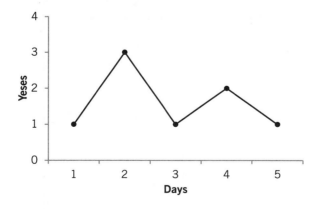

FIGURE 3.5. Baseline data aggregated by interval (top panel) and day (bottom panel) over 5 days.

obtained over the four intervals each day. This format is useful for determining whether there is indeed a problem. We address this issue in more detail in the next chapter.

To help you save time in keeping track of your data, we have created a spreadsheet in Excel, which you can use to store and chart baseline data. Purchasers can download this program at *www.guilford.com/volpe-forms*. The program allows the user to enter baseline data as raw frequencies or percentages (e.g., for percent of homework completed), and automatically makes a number of relevant calculations and charts the data for use in the DRC Design Interview. In this spreadsheet we have allowed room to enter data for up to eight target behaviors across up to 10 intervals (e.g., class periods).

The data you see charted in Figure 3.6 are Sky's baseline data for inappropriate noises. In the top panel the data charted represent the raw frequencies by day and setting. We decided to use a bar graph format here, given the potential number of settings. If we had used a line chart instead, the chart might have become a bit busy for users charting data across many settings, since lines would frequently overlap. The type of chart can easily be changed, however. In Excel for Windows, double-click the chart you want to change. This activates the "Design Menu." In the top left corner of your screen click on the "Change Chart Type" icon and select the format you prefer. On a Macintosh click the chart once and then click on the "Charts" tab at the top of your screen. In the top-left corner of your screen click on the "Change Chart Type" and select the type of chart you would like.

The middle panel is a chart graphing the average frequency of inappropriate noises for Sky across the 5 days of data collection for each interval (reading, writing, math, and science). You will notice that there are five 0's at the right end of the x-axis of this chart and the one above it. These 0's indicate that we could have entered data for five more target behaviors. To the left of the 0's we have used "Once a day" for the homework item of Sky's DRC. It is rated only once a day, and these data indicate that she did not turn in her homework on any of the 5 days. In the bottom panel, baseline data for inappropriate noises are charted in a time series. To generate this chart it is necessary first to enter the goal of the relevant target behavior. This would not be established until after the DRC Design Interview described in the next chapter. In this example we have entered seven as the goal, and as you can see, Sky would have earned half of her points for making fewer than seven inappropriate noises each of the 5 days during baseline. If you have a look at the top panel in Figure 3.6, it is easy to see that Sky would have earned 2 points in math and science each day but 0 points in reading and writing, because in those classes she made at least seven inappropriate noises each day.

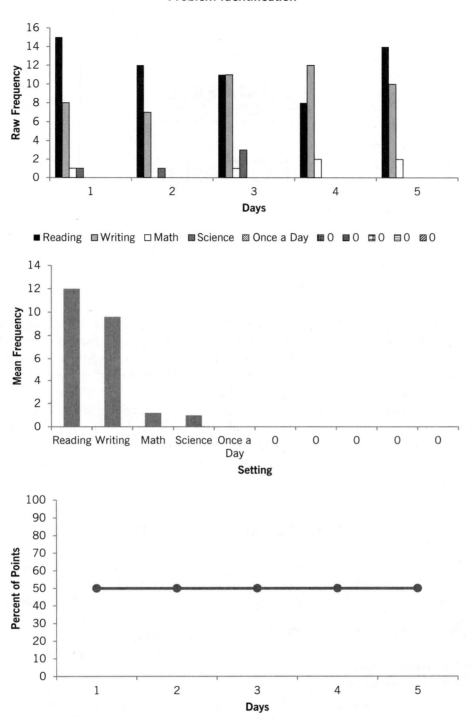

FIGURE 3.6. Sample charts from baseline data tool.

CHAPTER 4

DRC Design

Following screening, the initial meeting with the teacher to review the screening results, the Problem Identification Interview, and the collection of baseline data, the intervention team is ready to begin designing, constructing, and establishing a DRC intervention. Although in one sense this is a straightforward process—establish goals and criteria, format the goals on a DRC, and begin using the intervention—a number of considerations go into implementing an effective DRC intervention. The objectives of the DRC Design Interview are to create the DRC form (including the goals for each item) and identify the procedures for implementation and evaluation of the intervention. In this chapter we guide you through the process of conducting the DRC Design Interview and discuss some parameters that merit consideration during the DRC design phase.

THE DRC DESIGN INTERVIEW

Appendix H includes the DRC Design Interview Form. This form can be used to guide you through the DRC construction process. The steps in the DRC Design Interview include (1) a review of baseline data, (2) the establishment of target behaviors, (3) a determination of the frequency of ratings, (4) a discussion of the reward program for the DRC, (5) establishing procedures for progress monitoring, and (6) planning for maintenance and follow-up. Although the form is designed to efficiently guide the consultant through the process of designing the DRC, an interviewer could easily include additional questions or lines of inquiry, should these be required for a particular case.

DRC DESIGN INTERVIEW STEPS

1. **Review baseline data.**
2. **Establish target behaviors.**
3. **Determine the frequency of ratings.**
4. **Discuss the reward program for the DRC.**
5. **Establish procedures for progress monitoring.**
6. **Plan for maintenance and follow-up.**

FORMAT OF THE DRC FORM

Many roads lead to Rome when it comes to DRC formats, and as is discussed below, with the advent of technological advances, there are potentially new formats for DRCs that can be used in future efforts. The traditional DRC is a piece of paper with behavioral goals listed and a space for the teacher to provide an evaluation. It is also possible that space can be added for a parent signature to ensure that parents review and monitor the DRC each day. Appendix E provides multiple examples of DRCs and basic DRC templates. DRCs can be formatted differently, on the basis of the developmental level of the child and the purpose. We discuss each of these factors in turn.

Young children (preschool and early primary grades) often cannot read, and they also typically do not understand concepts such as percentage of targets met. For this reason, it is usually advisable to construct the format of the DRC in a manner that is useful to both the adults and children involved in the intervention. When working with a preschool child with high-functioning autism, we once took a set of pictures of the child sitting appropriately in circle time, walking in the hallway, and playing nicely with the other children in the class. During each half-hour activity, the child had three copies of each picture attached to a small clipboard. Every time he broke a rule, the teacher walked over and pointed to the picture, saying, "You need to use walking feet in the hallway" or "We sit down on our spot on the rug during circle time." Then, the picture was removed. The child earned a brief free-time period at the end of the activity to play with a preferred toy if he had at least one of each picture remaining. Other examples of this same principle include using "smiley faces" and "frowning faces" (or a neutral face, if preferred) for

> ## DEVELOPMENTAL CONSIDERATIONS
>
> 1. **Does the child understand the targets?**
> 2. **Does the child understand how feedback will work?**
> 3. **Does the child know how rewards are earned?**
> 4. **Is the feedback frequent enough?**
> 5. **Does the reward occur frequently enough?**

each target or goal, with the teacher verbally reviewing the written goal before and after each evaluation period (McGoey & DuPaul, 2000). Tokens that represent meeting goals in a reward approach or that are taken away when a target behavior is observed in a response–cost approach may also be important additions to the format of a DRC for young children.

For elementary school-age children, a traditional paper-and-pencil version of the DRC may be most appropriate. It is important for parents and teachers to ensure that the child understands the format, and what he or she needs to do to achieve daily goals; for instance, if the child meets 75–80% of the daily goals. Emphasizing the percentage may make it difficult for some children to track progress throughout the day. Rather than tell a child he or she needs to meet 75% of goals, a teacher could tell the child how many "yeses" are needed to get to 75%. Practically speaking, for a DRC with 16 possible "yeses," a teacher should tell the child that the daily goal is to earn 12 yeses or more. Using this approach, the child can easily count and monitor his or her progress toward the goal without being asked to perform complex mathematical calculations.

It is also a good idea to think about how to format the DRC so as to maximize the chances it will make it through the day in one piece and get back and forth from the child's home. Some teachers find placing the DRC in a sturdy binder or folder is helpful, whereas others may choose to place a small version of the DRC in a sleeve taped to the child's desk. Others have placed the

DRC on their own clipboard so that they could carry it with them throughout the classroom, and they can also hand it off to others (e.g., consultant teachers, special class teachers, cafeteria monitors) throughout the day.

An additional consideration in regard to format relates to record keeping. In problem-solving communication models, data-based decision making is emphasized. In fact, many child study or intervention teams within schools will consider only those cases for which baseline and ongoing data are collected. Many educators have found a benefit in writing their DRCs on carbon paper. As they tear off the top portion to send home with the child, they can save the bottom portion as a daily indicator of progress. In this way, the teacher maintains a running record of the child's behavioral progress on the targets, has a built-in track record to note changes (e.g., date when the DRC goals were modified; dates when the child was with a substitute), and is also equipped with ongoing data that can be used to inform multidisciplinary team decisions. We provide a detailed discussion of progress monitoring in Chapter 7.

As children move to middle school or high school, the format of the DRC may change further. Most students at these grade levels have an agenda or daily planner with them in each class. For these students, if a DRC is required, it is often preferable to write the targets on the bottom of each day/week in their planner. Sometimes, labels that list the targets can be printed, and these can simply be placed on the planner to be completed by the teacher. Because the planner typically travels to each of the classes across a teaching team, teachers can quickly make a note or evaluative mark in it related to the behavioral target (and also at the same time monitor whether the student has recorded the correct homework assignment). An additional consideration for older children is whether a physical DRC is necessary throughout the school day. It is possible that technological advances may promote home and school communication in a similar manner. In order to implement a DRC procedure for a middle school student, a parent and teaching team could establish a set of DRC goals (e.g., "Arrive on time for class"; "Be prepared with all materials"; "Have no instances of disrespectful behavior"). Then the parent could e-mail the teaching team each day and ask whether the teen met the targets. Teachers could e-mail back their report, as well as any additional comments. Variations of this approach include a school counselor or teaching team leader compiling reports each day and sending them to the parent. This approach may have the advantage of taking the preteen or teen out of the role of messenger, which may remove the temptation to forge information or "forget" to obtain teacher information, and it may also be less stigmatizing for the individual, as the other students would not be aware of the electronic communication taking place between parents and teachers. Further studies and field applications are likely needed to determine the merit of this approach, but it appears to be a promising one for working with older students.

FREQUENCY OF FEEDBACK

The first decision that needs to be made by the implementers of the DRC is how often the targets will be evaluated by the teacher. In our experience working in schools we have seen DRC targets evaluated as frequently as every few minutes and for spans as long as a week. To some degree the periods between evaluations will be determined by the frequency of feedback needed by the child, the teacher's time, and the nature of the target behavior. It is also possible that the evaluation periods may change over time. An excellent program developed by Hill

Walker and Hyman Hops is the Contingencies for Learning and School Success (CLASS) program (e.g., Walker & Hops, 1979; Walker, Retana, & Gersten, 1988). This program was developed for working with students who have significant challenging behaviors (aggression, disruptive behaviors, etc.). In the CLASS program, teachers initially partner with another person such as a school psychologist, classroom aide, or other paraprofessional. The helper has a card that is red on one side and green on the other. Whenever the child is following the classroom rules, the green card is displayed to the child. However, if the child engages in rule-breaking behavior, he or she is shown the red side of the card, which remains until the child exhibits appropriate behavior again. During the class, the helper is prompted to mark whether the child is following rules during randomly selected time intervals. At the end of the class, if the child was on "green" for enough of the intervals, a reward or privilege is provided. Over time, the child is asked to exhibit appropriate behavior more often and over longer intervals. Eventually, once the child's behavior has improved to a considerable degree, the program is transferred to the teacher for monitoring and evaluation—but the teacher does not have to provide feedback as often due to the child's improvement. The CLASS program demonstrates how a DRC intervention can be initiated with initial support, even for children with considerable behavioral challenges.

Educators should consider a few key principles when deciding on the latency of feedback, however. Some of these principles are best illustrated by focusing on extremes in the provision of feedback. Take, for instance, a teacher who decides to provide feedback on the DRC at the end of the week, albeit in such cases one likely would not call the method a DRC at all. For a child who is well behaved all through the week, or a child who misbehaves consistently throughout the week, this teacher's job is easy. However, most children who exhibit the classroom behaviors or need for academic accommodations that result in a DRC rarely behave so consistently. In fact, the hallmark of children with behavioral difficulties in school is that they are so inconsistent—a pattern that makes teachers and parents all the more frustrated because they see appropriate behavior some days, yet inappropriate behavior on others. Thus, a weekly DRC behavioral summary might be quite difficult for a teacher to put together. For instance, how would a teacher respond to the target "Followed classroom rules" if the child was well behaved Monday, needed four or five reminders to stay in his seat Tuesday, was in the office all day Wednesday serving an in-school suspension for fighting in the cafeteria, followed rules on Thursday, and then again needed reminders to be respectful on Friday after arguing during a partner assignment? Considering this situation, the teacher might have quite a bit of difficulty capturing all that information in a "yes–no" response or 1–5 rating. Or consider a child who has a tough day on Monday with respect to behavior and/or academic productivity. If this child knows or suspects on Monday afternoon that she is going to get a negative DRC report on Friday, she may decide to "get her money's worth" and reduce her effort in behavior and academics for the rest of the week. Furthermore, a weekly report removes the opportunity for the teacher to provide positive, supportive, and corrective feedback to the child throughout the week. For all these reasons, weekly reports are typically used only in rare cases or after long-term use of a DRC wherein the feedback can gradually be faded from daily to weekly intervals.

In contrast to a weekly report, frequent feedback on the order of every few minutes may result in different problems in a typical general education classroom (such frequent feedback is certainly feasible in situations where an aide or paraprofessional may be present to implement the program). The problem with this type of setup is that it may be nearly impossible for a teacher to implement the plan consistently. Clearly, inconsistent implementation of a plan may be even worse than doing nothing at all, as it may send the wrong message to the student and his or her parents. In the long run, setting up these "impossible missions" may also decrease teachers' investment in DRCs, which would also be an unfortunate consequence.

For the reasons outlined above, best practice typically requires teachers to evaluate DRC goals at least twice a day, and more often if the teacher is able and if doing so would be appropriate for the targeted behavior. Some goals lend themselves to multiple evaluations throughout the day due to their nature—a child may have an academic seatwork completion target that is evaluated after reading, English/language arts, math, and writing (i.e., four evaluations/day). Other goals may be evaluated only once a day; for instance, behavior on the morning bus; during a "special" class such as physical education, art, or music; or in the cafeteria during lunch. Finally, some targets may need to be evaluated only once per day. For instance, a child who only has difficulty completing math worksheets on time, or cooperating with a partner during science class, should only have these behaviors observed and evaluated within the situations where problems are present.

SETUP AND IMPLEMENTATION CONSIDERATIONS

Although it seems like a minor detail, it is important when establishing a DRC to think through details related to implementation and setup. These might include determining who will type up and copy the DRC, who will review the DRC with the child at the beginning of each day, how feedback on progress toward DRC goals will be provided within the classroom, what the reward menu will look like, and how often the team will meet to monitor and evaluate progress. These issues are best addressed before the first DRC is actually implemented to ensure proper administration of the intervention.

Educators should take care to ensure that the goals are defined in a way that is specific enough for everyone to understand and evaluate. In situations where a teacher has a clearly operationalized set of classroom rules, a target related to following rules with only a certain number of reminders would be appropriate. In contrast, in situations where the class rules are vague or applied inconsistently, a specific target for each rule would be preferable. It is also often helpful to review the targets with the child initially, role-play good/bad examples of what the targets are, and then review the targets at the beginning of each day and throughout the day as needed. This repetition serves to ensure that the child comprehends the goals and is mindful of them throughout the day. A good rule of thumb when setting goals is to ensure that if 10 different teachers watched a particular behavior, all 10 would classify the behavior in the same way. If there is any room for disagreement, this may be a cue that the target behavior needs to be more clearly defined.

DRCs THAT USE SPECIFIC BEHAVIORAL CRITERIA

Sometimes teachers use DRCs that require students to meet general expectations, such as following classroom rules or completing all work assigned. These versions of DRCs are often useful for whole-class implementation because they cover typical classroom expectations, and the broad definitions used capture a host of relevant behaviors. For instance, Pelham, Massett, and colleagues (2005) reported on an efficient and effective procedure for using daily positive home notes for an entire elementary school. In this school, teachers had precopied notes that they gave to children at dismissal if they returned completed homework, followed all rules, and obtained a parent signature on the homework assignment sheet from the prior evening. Parents were asked at the beginning of the school year to check with their children each day for the presence of the positive notes, display them prominently at home, and provide positive consequences/rewards to their children for bringing home positive notes each afternoon. Similar procedures have been observed in our work in schools where teachers have an existing classwide behavior modification system, such as the traffic light system. A laminated figure of a traffic light and movable nametags for each student can be used to provide feedback to students on their classroom behavior. At the beginning of each school day, nametags for each student are placed in a neutral area and can be moved next to the green light for good behavior, next to the yellow light if they need warnings during the day, and next to the red light for repeated warnings or egregious violations of school rules. In some classrooms, children put a green, yellow, or red dot in their assignment notebook/agenda each day, and parents see this behavioral feedback when they view the assigned homework each evening. This simple and efficient approach also provides general daily feedback to parents.

For many children in general education settings, this form of home–school communication is likely to be sufficient because typically developing students follow school rules, return completed homework, and remember parent signatures most of the time. For students with behavioral or academic challenges, however, it is likely that a more intensive approach will be required that includes clear definitions of specific target behaviors. For instance, a typical child with behavioral challenges may have poor insight into the impact his or her behaviors have on the classroom, the teacher, or even on him- or herself. If it were as easy as telling the child to stop doing the behaviors that cause trouble and start doing more of the behaviors that are adaptive, indeed no DRC would be needed.

For this reason, DRCs that clearly spell out expectations are often helpful for children who require improvement across a range of behaviors. There was a good example of this in a case one of us worked on during graduate school (see Fabiano & Pelham, 2003). In this case, the teachers had really done a great job, by all accounts, with the student, but he was just not improving in his behavior. They had listed a number of goals for the child to meet during each class period, and after each class the teacher met briefly with the child to discuss whether he had been successful in meeting his goals. These goals were "Finish work in the time provided"; "Follow directions"; "Work quietly"; "Cooperate with peers and adults"; and "Stay on task." There was no dispute over the behaviors included in these goals, but the child's teachers reported that when they sat down to review whether the child met the goals during each class period, he always said he did—which often did not match the teachers' perceptions. In this case, a simple way to operationalize the child's goals was to add a "three strikes and you're out criteria." If the child needed more than two warnings for any of the goals, that goal was considered to be unmet. This clarified the expectations across these goals for the child *and* the teachers, and it resulted in better classroom behavior almost immediately. The clarification of the limits for meeting or not meeting a goal likely helped the child and the teachers implement the DRC plan in a more consistent and therefore effective way.

DRCs THAT USE A RATING SYSTEM

In contrast to the behavioral criteria described above, some DRCs use a rating system, whereby students are rated on a scale. Barkley (1997) provides a good example of this type of approach in which a child is rated on a 5-point scale ranging from *excellent* to *very poor*. There has been some thought that this type of approach may introduce an unnecessary need for judgment into the completion of DRCs; however, a recent meta-analysis suggested that for some students this may be a more effective approach. Vannest, Davis, Davis, Mason, and Burke (2010) reviewed research studies that used a DRC for students with behavioral problems. Because the meta-analysis included 17 different studies, they could look across studies for findings that were consistent across the different investigations and classrooms. One interesting finding was that better outcomes were obtained when teachers used a target that had a more qualitative indicator (teachers were given an example of meeting or not meeting a goal and then judged what should be rated for the child) as compared to a more formal indicator, such as the number of times a student called out (cf. Riley-Tillman, Chafouleas, Christ, Briesch, & LeBel, 2009). On the surface, this finding is puzzling, as the frequency counts are more precise. However, it is possible that teachers have more difficulty counting the behaviors and recording them on the DRC consistently, which makes this approach less practical and therefore less effective in classroom settings. Perhaps in this case the sacrifice in accuracy is worth the increase in consistency, which promotes the greater effectiveness of the qualitative ratings.

A related approach that uses a rating of behavior is called a direct behavior rating (DBR; *http://directbehaviorratings.com/cms*). A DBR is completed by observing a child for a specified period of time and then rating the percentage of time the child was on-task, respectful, and disruptive. These ratings have been used in multiple investigations that show they are useful for progress monitoring as well as for intervention (e.g., a child could receive a reward at home or at school for achieving positive ratings on a DBR). More detail is provided on this method in Chapter 7.

DRCs WITH SCHOOL- VERSUS HOME-BASED REWARDS

Many DRCs have a reward component integrated into their application. This is an approach that is widely used across different aspects of our society. For instance, supermarket loyalty programs may ask a user to "swipe" a card every time the person shops, and after spending $100 the individual may earn a free coupon toward groceries. The traditional punch clock at worksites also targets the behavior of "being at work on time and for the expected duration," and a paycheck at the end of the week based on the data collected by the punch clock is the linked reward.

Using the same basic principles, the DRC can provide structure for school- or home-based rewards. O'Leary and Pelham (1978) described a DRC intervention for hyperactive youth wherein parents rewarded success on DRC targets at home each afternoon. It is interesting in the description of methods for this study that out of the seven children included in the study, three needed additional modifications made to the DRC plan. For instance, one child did not respond by showing improvement in the behaviors targeted once the DRC was implemented.

The clinicians determined that the child (a third grader) could not delay gratification until the end of the day when rewards were provided by the parent. In this case, the teacher provided the child with a coupon for 5 minutes of television time immediately after meeting one of the DRC goals (i.e., completing a daily seatwork assignment), and this reward helped the child improve his performance in class.

Teachers may also choose to provide in-school rewards or privileges based on DRC performance. This is likely done informally in many classrooms using contingency management (e.g., "When you finish your seatwork, then you can go to free play"). However, a DRC can also be used to inform school rewards. Teachers may choose to take away privileges that used to be provided noncontingently, such as recess or free play, and base access to these preferred activities on a DRC performance that is satisfactory. School rewards were also based on positive home notes in Pelham and colleagues' (2008) schoolwide behavioral program. In this school, children could go to a "fun Friday" activity such as a nature walk, sports competition, or arts and crafts activity if they earned four out of five possible positive daily notes during the week.

DRCs WITH RESPONSE COST

Often rewards are insufficient to promote positive behaviors. If rewards alone were sufficient for promoting appropriate behaviors, there would be no reason for parking/traffic tickets, high school detention, or fines for National Football League players who celebrate "too much" following a touchdown. The same holds true for some children when DRCs are implemented, and some research illustrates that a response cost procedure (i.e., taking away rewards/privileges) can be a useful addition to a DRC that includes a reward program. McCain and Kelley (1994) demonstrated that a response cost component of a DRC can be a useful addition. Specifically, teachers provided feedback on DRC targets throughout the class period. Each DRC also had five smiley faces printed on the bottom. Each time the teacher saw the child engage in off-task or disruptive behavior, she instructed the child to cross out one of the smiley faces. The number of smiley faces left at the end of the day factored into the rewards provided by parents in the evening and also served as a concrete way for the children to monitor their behavior throughout the day. The investigators showed that three 11-year-old children, referred for serious levels of disruptive behavior, responded best to a DRC that included a reward component combined with a response cost component.

ADDITIONAL CONSIDERATIONS

An additional consideration when constructing DRC goals is that each should have a criterion. In Chapter 3 we discussed the importance of collecting baseline data in order to inform the accurate construction of behavioral criteria for the targeted behaviors on the DRC. The criterion provides a limit or identifies a behavioral product that will help the teacher, child, and parent know whether the behavioral goal was met or not. Sometimes this criterion involves simply stating the goal with a clause at the end that says "with three or fewer reminders," or "with five or fewer instances." For academic completion targets, a criterion related to the percent of problems completed accurately and the amount of work completed is advisable. These criteria are important for a few reasons. First, they preclude the often difficult situation of making a judgment call on whether or not the child met the goal for the day. If the teacher counts the number of times a behavior occurred or corrects work assignments in a typical manner, he or she is simply evaluating performance. By adding a criterion, the teacher can also provide consistent feedback to the child throughout the day and across days. There is also an advantage to this approach for the child. The child can keep track of the feedback received from the teacher throughout the day, and some will actively modify behavior based on the performance toward daily goals. For instance, a child who has a target that states "interrupt class discussions after two or fewer reminders" may actively inhibit his or her impulsive interruptions during a class discussion after receiving two reminders from the teacher. A child with a target to initiate three contributions to a classroom discussion may also keep track of the number of contributions made during a 40-minute class period as he or she works toward the goal.

A final consideration when establishing goals and a criterion for each relates to the attainability of the goals. Most DRCs are established in response to problematic levels of behavior that deviate significantly from classroom norms, and, understandably, there is often a feeling of urgency to improve behavior quickly. However, it is important for all invested parties to remember that behavioral change is typically a slow process, and that it most often occurs in small, incremental steps. It is also important, from the perspective of the child, for the DRC to be a positive intervention. This means that individuals who are setting the goals on the DRC should ensure that they are attainable. To use an exaggerated example, for a child who is completing no seatwork at all, there may be a desire to set a goal of completing *all* assigned work. However, such a sweeping goal will likely set up the child for failure—to go from completing *no* work to completing *all* work is an unlikely situation (if it were that easy, a DRC would not be needed!). A more reasonable approach would be to identify small, positive steps toward the goal of completing all seatwork, and as progress is made at each step, teachers can make the goals more difficult so that the child is continually challenged to improve toward the *eventual* goal of 100% completion.

Related to the issue of setting of attainable goals is the need to modify goals as the DRC is implemented (see discussion of progress monitoring in Chapter 7). Although hopefully educators are in the position of making goals more challenging as a child demonstrates consistent success, sometimes goals may need to be more liberal in order to ensure success. As a general benchmark, children should earn "yeses" on 70–80% of goals each day. If a child is earning a lower percentage of affirmative marks for 3 to 4 days in a row, one option is to make the criteria less stringent so that the child improves his or her success rate.

One consideration with setting attainable goals is that it is always preferable to make goals a little tougher, based on success, rather than making goals easier based on failure. For this reason, educators should think carefully about the criteria for the initial targets they set for a child. Absent clear guidance from baseline data or other sources of information, it may be advisable to set targets at an initially "easy" level. This will help get the DRC off to a positive start, and it may also help build the child and parent's confidence in the intervention. After a day or two, these goals could be modified to more difficult levels based on the child's current performance.

Setting DRC Targets for Sky

We can use the DRC Design Interview framework to illustrate the construction of one of Sky's DRC targets. We have previously discussed (1) how to identify Sky as a student in need of a DRC through screening (Chapter 2) and (2) the collection of baseline data for her identified behaviors (Chapter 3). Now we discuss the approach for identifying and quantifying her target behaviors.

To use an example, Figure 3.6 (p. 31) lists Sky's frequency counts of inappropriate, disruptive noises. The baseline data provide some useful information to discuss during the DRC Design Interview. For this behavior, there are sufficient baseline data—5 days of observations were conducted. The information also is presented across classes, which leads to a logical conclusion. Sky has trouble with this behavior during reading and writing class, but it is not occurring at abnormal levels in her other classes. Thus, the teacher and consultant would likely decide to target this behavior on the DRC only for the two classes where the behavior is exhibited to a disruptive degree (reading and writing). Further, the behavior is exhibited an average of 12 times per day in reading and about 10 times per day in writing. The discussion during the DRC Design Interview leads the consultant to believe that Sky might be capable of attaining a modest reduction of this problematic behavior at the start of the DRC intervention. Therefore, the goals are set with a 20% reduction of the behavior in mind. This results in a target of "Makes 10 or fewer inappropriate noises during reading" and "Makes 8 or fewer inappropriate noises during writing." In subsequent chapters we discuss how to establish home reward programs and monitoring procedures.

CHAPTER 5

Explaining the DRC to Students

Once the DRC is constructed, an important next step is to explain the DRC to the child. This explanation will need to be straightforward and developmentally appropriate. For instance, we can recall a well-meaning school counselor who was describing the DRC to a kindergartener by saying that he just needed to earn 75% of his goals in order to earn a reward at lunchtime and the end of the day. Unfortunately, this boy could not fluently count to 10. There is no way he understood what *75% of goals met* meant! In this case, a developmentally appropriate approach may have been to use some kind of visual prompt (e.g., poker chips, marbles in a jar; see suggestions below) to scaffold the child's understanding of progress toward DRC goals.

DRC interventions can be effective for preschoolers, elementary-age students, middle school students, and even high school students. However, as illustrated in the example above, one critical consideration in describing the DRC to a student is a careful consideration of his or her developmental level. Because of different levels of cognitive, linguistic, and attentional abilities, it is very important to think about each child's capacity and level when developing the intervention. For instance, for preschool and elementary-age children, frequent feedback throughout the day is likely to be necessary in almost all cases. In contrast, high school students might be able to achieve goals with feedback provided less frequently. Indeed, middle and high school students may find it very unappealing to have a teacher provide feedback on a DRC in front of the class. In these cases it is recommended that the teacher and student develop a brief feedback mechanism that is generally private (e.g., recording DRC progress in the agenda at the student's desk).

When explaining the DRC to the child, it is also important to ensure that the overall tone of the presentation is positive. Most times, by the time the child is having a DRC explained, the child (and parent) has already had a number of failure experiences that have led up to the current point. Therefore, it is advisable to emphasize that the DRC goals are ones the child is able to meet, the teacher is going to help keep the child on track toward the goals, and the child will be earning rewards based on behavioral performance. Often, emphasizing the opportunities to earn rewards and privileges is a good way to help the child buy into the program. It is also important for adults to ensure that their tone and approach are encouraging and supportive. Sarcasm, negative tone, or dwelling on past failure experiences are communication "strategies" to avoid.

Behavior contracts are an effective strategy to enhance the cooperation and commitment of stakeholders (e.g., Lane, Menzies, Bruhn, & Crnobori, 2011). We have created a DRC contract that specifies the roles of the teacher, parent, and student (Appendix G). Reviewing and initialing this form together makes explicit the role of each stakeholder and affirms their commitment to the procedures.

LEVEL OF CHILD INVOLVEMENT

Given that children at times have poor insight into their problematic behaviors (if they had better insight, it is unlikely there would be a reason for a DRC intervention), it is important for professionals to introduce key targets and facilitate their inclusion on the DRC, even if the youth does not bring a potential target to the discussion. Thus, children should be involved in the process of establishing DRC targets, but the adults involved in the process should take care to remain in the driver's seat in any discussions. Children are likely to take much larger roles in a task with proximal interest to them following the creation of DRC targets—the establishment of home-based rewards (see discussion below).

It should be acknowledged that children's involvement in the process of establishing DRC goals will vary based on the age of the child. Although younger children may be involved in the process of discussing DRC goals, for the most part the creation of goals should be directed through the conversations of the teacher, parent, and other school professionals. However, as children progress to the middle and high school levels, they might be important contributors to the process of defining and creating goals. In fact, including youth in this stage of the process may enhance buy-in for the program, as the student feels that he or she had some control over the process of establishing the DRC. It is possible that the inclusion of older youth in these discussions supports the development of self-determination and self-management skills (see Chapter 8).

It is also important for the adults involved in the process to be cognizant of whether a child's contributions are helpful to the overall plan. In some cases where there have been long-standing behavior problems or school failure experiences, it may even be helpful to begin with easier goals (those that the student is likely to meet). The goals can then be made more difficult relatively quickly, but the advantage is that the child has experienced success, which can lead to more motivation with respect to the program. Although it does not happen all the time, our clinical experience has been that in some cases a child that has a few successful experiences starts behaving like all the other children in the classroom quickly—all that was needed was the opportunity for the child to realize that he or she could meet the targets successfully. When we ask children directly about goals, we find that they sometimes overestimate their ability to meet strict behavioral goals, and therefore it is important to make this process collaborative, yet sensible.

TEACHER SUPPORT FOR CHILD INVOLVEMENT

Well-operationalized DRC targets are a clear component of DRCs (see Chapters 3 and 4). The reason for clear operalization of goals is to ensure that the teacher, parent, and child understand what is being addressed on the DRC. Prior to implementing the DRC, the teacher should review the targets with the child and explain them in a concrete way. This might include verbal descriptions of targeted behaviors or more intensive approaches such as role plays. In our clinical experience we've often used verbal explanations of inappropriate behaviors that would result in missing a DRC target, and then we have asked the child to role-play an incompatible, positive alternative to the inappropriate behavior. For instance, for a target related to being out of seat, the child might be asked to show what it means to be in an assigned seat or area. The child can then walk over to his or her desk, sit down, and face the front of the classroom. By having the child role-play each of the behaviors that is consistent with meeting the DRC goals, the teacher is providing multiple opportunities to praise and encourage the child during this practice routine, the child is able to demonstrate his or her capacity for meeting the goals, and the DRC intervention is launched off of a solid base of clear expectations and understanding.

Teachers can also support continued child involvement as the DRC program is started. Even if it takes just 30 seconds, teachers should review DRC goals with the child as soon as he or she enters the classroom (and before getting off on the wrong foot). This informal meeting should include a brief reminder of DRC goals, some questions related to whether home-based rewards were provided the previous evening, and encouragement and support related to the teacher's belief that the child will be successful during the upcoming school day. If a child had an unsuccessful time the prior day, the teacher may also find it helpful to remind the child that he or she has a clean slate and can start the day off on a good foot by again working toward meeting the goals. If the child had a successful day the previous day, then the teacher can use this result as an opportunity to reinforce the child's positive behavior and encourage him or her to continue to work in a positive direction. Many children will have goals evaluated during various time periods (e.g., A.M./P.M.; for each subject area; different goals for the cafeteria, specials, and/or lunch). For these cases, it is important that teachers review the expectations and goals for these time periods prior to their start. This review helps the child remain mindful of behavioral expectations throughout the day.

Children can also be involved in the daily tracking and accounting of DRC goals met by monitoring their own progress throughout the day. Some teachers find it helpful to tape a small reminder sheet to children's desks that lists the daily goals for each class period. Children can then make small tick marks or cross out a mark that represents a warning regarding a DRC objective (e.g., a goal of "Five or fewer interruptions" might have that goal listed with five

---

MORNING MEETING BETWEEN THE CHILD AND TEACHER

1. Review goals/targets for the day.

2. Check in and see whether rewards were provided appropriately the day before.

3. Encourage and validate the child's ability to meet goals during the upcoming day.

   a. If the prior day was a rough one, remind the child that the new day has a clean slate.

   b. If the prior day was a good one, encourage the child to build on the prior day's success.

circles next to it). In this way, each child has an ongoing reminder of his or her progress toward goals. An additional benefit of this approach to keeping the child involved in the DRC process is that the tracking sheet can be used by the teacher to account for whether the child met the goals or not without any additional note taking. Some teachers (provided good oversight) might also have the child circle the yeses and nos on the DRC throughout the day and sign off at the end of the day after checking for accuracy.

PARENT SUPPORT FOR CHILD INVOLVEMENT

It is also important to think about student involvement as persisting throughout the duration of DRC implementation. Although the program might be obvious to the adults, it is advisable to review the DRC with the child each morning (even if this takes just a few moments), and to revisit the DRC throughout the day and even before bedtime. Parents should review the reward list with the child as he or she gets on the bus or gets dropped off at school to make sure that the child is attending to the program and remembers the consequences of both positive and negative behaviors during the school day. Parents should also create a home-based routine wherein the DRC is reviewed as soon as the child and parent are home together. This review should be consistent across days. Parents should be enthusiastic and attentive to goals that are met each day. For goals that are not met, parents should be neutral and refrain from lecturing or reprimanding. (Presumably these are things parents have tried before moving to a DRC intervention, and if they worked, once again, there would be no reason to start a DRC in the first place!). Being mindful of the DRC as a positive-focused intervention, most attention should be directed toward success. Using the same approach, rewards should be provided with great fanfare, whereas unearned privileges should be addressed matter-of-factly.

PROVIDING EFFECTIVE FEEDBACK ON PROGRESS

Hopefully, most instances of DRC-related feedback provided to the child are positive. However, at times, the feedback may need to describe shortfalls related to goal attainment. Because of this, it is wise for teachers to establish regular, private meetings to give DRC feedback. This might involve a quiet conversation at the teacher's or student's desk, a quick meeting at a back table in the classroom, or some other arrangement. It is also important to ensure that these interactions are quick. If lecturing resulted in behavior change for most children involved in a DRC intervention, a DRC would not be needed to begin with! These feedback discussions should be positive, straightforward, and solution-focused (as opposed to dwelling on problems). If the child missed a goal or goals, that feedback should be brief and neutral in tone. The brief discussion should end with a prompt that the child can now begin working

Interactions with students should be . . .
1. **Quick.**
2. **Clear.**
3. **Focused on the positive.**
4. **Delivered in a neutral tone when addressing negative behavior.**

toward meeting the next set of goals, and the teacher can encourage the child to start working right away.

STUDENT FEEDBACK

It may also be advisable to ask the child, along the way, how the program is working for him or her. It is possible that the child may have suggestions that will result in quality improvements that will promote the continued use and success of the program. For instance, we once worked with a middle school student who was asked to bring his agenda up to the teacher at the end of class to have the goals marked as met or not. In the class, typically many students attempted to talk to the teacher, and this resulted in the child falling behind and being late for the next class. Because the student was working hard to meet the DRC goals, and being on time for class was one of them, this situation was distressing to him. Fortunately, the student volunteered this information as a problem, and the teacher was readily able to solve it by prioritizing his feedback at the end of class before dealing with other student issues. Children may also help sound alarm bells if they comment on lack of rewards at home or reveal that they do not like a current reward. These comments should cue parents and teachers that the reward menu needs revision.

Throughout the DRC intervention, parents and teachers should check in with the child and comment on their satisfaction with the child's performance. These interactions also provide a forum for the child to offer feedback or comments regarding his or her view of the DRC intervention as well as their school performance. It is also an opportunity to ask the child to think and talk about some of the areas in which he or she has demonstrated improvement or growth. Adults should listen carefully to these contributions and definitely reinforce and praise the child's efforts!

EXPLAINING THE DRC TO SKY

Sky's teacher has constructed a DRC, and she is ready to explain the DRC intervention to her. To do this, Sky's teacher arranged for her to come down to the classroom 10 minutes early from the morning program Sky attends before school. The teacher greets Sky warmly as she comes in and asks her to have a seat at the big table at the back of the room. Sky's teacher starts by saying, "I am really proud of your work this year in my class, and I think you've really grown in your reading and writing skills. I like how you work hard in class. At the same time, I think you'll agree that we have some areas we need to keep working on. Do you have an idea about some behaviors you and I might focus on improving?"

Sky replies, "Well, I know I have been getting in trouble for talking too much."

"I'd agree with that," her teacher says. "In fact, talking too much and talking disrespectfully are both things you and I have been talking about a lot lately."

Sky nods.

Sky's teacher continues, "Well, Sky, we are going to try something called a 'daily report card.' This daily report card is going to give you some goals each day—to keep your noises and talking back to fewer than eight times in the morning and afternoon, and it is also going to encourage you to complete your work without a lot of reminders from me."

Sky's teacher shows her the DRC and asks if she has any questions.

After Sky shakes her head, her teacher continues: "I know what I am asking you to do is going to take a lot of work. Because you are going to be working so hard to meet these goals, your mom and I talked about some special rewards you can earn if you meet most of your daily goals. Did your mom talk to you about this?"

"My mom said I would get to watch TV if I earned enough of my goals that day."

"That's right. When I talked to your mom, she said you'd get to watch two TV shows if you had an excellent day, almost all yeses, and one show for a pretty good day—about 10 yeses. Does this sound like something you can do?"

Sky smiles and nods her head yes. Her teacher reiterates that she is proud of Sky and confident that she can meet the goals. Her teacher then hands her the DRC and reminds her of each of the targets. Sky is also reminded to bring the DRC to the teacher before lunch and before she leaves for the bus line at the end of the day so that her teacher can fill it out.

CHAPTER 6

Working with Parents
Establishing a Home-Based Reward System

A cornerstone of the DRC intervention is the development and implementation of a home-based reward system. The importance of this aspect of the DRC intervention program cannot be underestimated. Imagine a situation in which a person on an assembly line meets the daily quota, but when opening his or her pay envelope at the end of the week, finds no paycheck. This person would be very likely to lose motivation, and production would suffer. The same holds true for children with DRCs. Thus, it is not sufficient to simply create the DRC targets and provide feedback to the child on progress. Perhaps the most important part of the DRC intervention is the implementation of home-based rewards/privileges that are contingent on DRC success. This was noted as a crucial component of the intervention by Jon Bailey in one of the first DRC studies (Bailey et al., 1970). A recent study of DRCs investigated the correlates of DRC components with positive outcomes at the end of the year. The authors of the study found that how often the DRC was sent home by the teacher did not correlate with outcomes. However, consistent implementation of home-based rewards was significantly related to improved behavior at the end of the year (Fabiano et al., 2010). Indeed, home-based reinforcement of DRC goals appears to be the lynchpin of the intervention.

The importance of the home-based reinforcement cannot be emphasized enough. Yet, this is an area that educators report as one of the most difficult to implement successfully. Sometimes it is difficult to meet and coordinate with parents. Other times, parents may have difficulty providing home-based backups due to family schedules and the presence of multiple caretakers (e.g., babysitters, after-school programs). Further, some individuals may feel that rewards are not necessary to encourage positive behavior, or that rewarding children for acceptable behavior is incompatible with their values. It is also reasonable to say that sometimes DRCs are needed in spite of the family situation, which may be impaired to a degree that parents cannot provide consistent positive consequences because of other psychosocial stressors. Due to all these potential reasons we want to emphasize that there is no "one-size-fits-all" approach to home-based reinforcement, so the goal for consultants coordinating DRC is to establish the *best* home-based system possible, within the current family context. As we discuss below, in some situations, school-based rewards may be utilized in lieu of home-based rewards, if necessary.

There are several reasons why parent involvement in the DRC intervention is so important. Whereas teachers come and go, parents are typically consistent stakeholders throughout the child's school career, which makes them key agents for promoting consistency and effectiveness in interventions. Second, parents are in control of a large array of potential rewards in the home setting, far more than are typically available in the classroom. Indeed, if a parent provides noncontingent access to home-based rewards, most teachers would find it hard to make school-based rewards effective in this context. Third, parents can act as partners in monitoring how well the DRC is working, and the DRC serves as a way for teachers and parents to communicate in a positive way.

The function of positive communication through a DRC also cannot be overstated. For many parents of children who exhibit the types of behaviors that call for an intervention such as a DRC, positive communication with individuals from the school may be infrequent. It is possible that most notes in the child's backpack, combined with phone calls, meetings, and conferences, have focused on negative behaviors such as missing homework, incomplete work, poor grades, or comments about the child's disruptive or otherwise inappropriate behavior. In contrast, the DRC, with its positively phrased targets, sends the message that the child is being successful at school. Through positive daily correspondence, parents and teachers cultivate a collaborative relationship that proactively supports the child, rather than the more typical reactive feedback system that delivers only bad news. Over time, this background daily communication may help support more problem solving and adaptive coping on the part of the parent and school when unexpected problems arise. Teachers and school staff likely also appreciate the parents' contribution to the school program, and teachers' motivation to persist with a DRC intervention is typically greatest when parents contribute to the intervention as well.

Below we outline the steps involved in promoting parent involvement in the DRC intervention. In our experience this is the aspect of the intervention most often missing when DRCs are established. Schools must proactively strive to maximize parent involvement, and in some cases real creativity might be necessary. For instance, it is often difficult to hold a formal meeting with a working parent, teacher, and other school staff. Simple technologies such as conference calls or more innovative technologies such as videoconferencing often can address challenges in scheduling. Some parents may also be able to set up a home-based reward program with the Home Reward Planning Sheet (see Appendix F). If a parent cannot immediately take part in the DRC intervention by providing home rewards, sending the DRC home each day is still a means of promoting effective feedback and communication. In these cases, however, teachers will have to supplement the DRC with school-based rewards to promote effectiveness.

As mentioned above, prior to the initiation of a DRC, a parent has often received a considerable amount of negative feedback from the school. Thus, it is prudent to be mindful of this possible history when introducing the DRC. It is often helpful to acknowledge that the child has been having some recent struggles, but that the DRC is a way to increase confidence because it is intended to be a positive program. In fact, the only consequence that is negative is that a child may miss out on a reward on a particular day. However, the very next school day the child will have a clean slate and again be in an earning situation. To promote collaboration, parents might also be invited to review or contribute to the development of target behaviors. Similarly, teachers may find it helpful to have a copy of the parent's reward list so that the rewards can be reviewed with the child during the day and the reminders serve to focus the child's attention on the behaviors needed to meet the goals.

ESTABLISHING A HOME-BASED REWARD SYSTEM

Once parents agree to the DRC program, the key task is to establish home-based rewards for DRC performance. Effective home-based rewards are those the child is willing to exert effort to earn. Parents can identify effective rewards through multiple strategies including watching what the child does when given free choice, thinking about what the child would choose as a special privilege, or simply asking the child what he or she would like to earn. It is typically helpful to generate a long list of potential rewards, as the next step is to organize the rewards into a hierarchical menu.

WAYS TO ORGANIZE A REWARD MENU

1. **Group rewards by percentage of goals met (e.g., Level 1: 40–60%; Level 2: 61–80%; Level 3: 81–100%).**
2. **Establish levels of each reward based on percentage of goals met (e.g., 5 minutes of television or access to an activity for each goal met).**

The form in Appendix F lists some examples of rewards that might be placed on a reward menu. Figure 6.1 summarizes important considerations for selecting appropriate rewards. Parents might find it helpful to sit down with the child and circle the rewards the child indicates as desirable. Then parents should look at the circled rewards and decide whether there are any that should be taken "off the table." For instance, some parents might find it unpleasant to think about withholding a bedtime story if this is a special time they enjoy spending with the child each night. If the parent is not willing to withhold this activity if it is not earned, it should not be included on the list of potential reinforcers. Similarly, some rewards might not be applicable on a daily basis (e.g., going to the park, going out for ice cream). In these cases, the rewards could

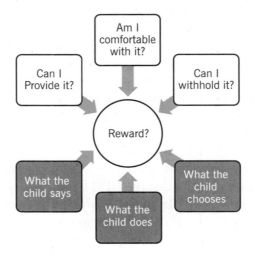

FIGURE 6.1. Choosing appropriate rewards.

be listed on the reward menu, but the parent would have to inform the child ahead of time when these particular rewards were not available to be selected.

A few thoughts about the rationale behind the reward menu might be helpful. It is very important that the reward list is a menu. McDonald's was put on the map because it served a really good hamburger, but as a business always focused on the bottom line, it knows that its customers are not always in the mood for a hamburger—sometimes they want chicken, or ice cream, or a salad (some people prefer a rib sandwich!). Some restaurants may even serve breakfast at dinnertime to cater to the preference of particular customers. An extensive menu helps ensure that anyone who comes into the restaurant finds something that is worth ordering. The same principle applies to DRC rewards—although TV might be a really powerful reward on Tuesdays when a particular show is on, Wednesday nights might not have the same lineup of programming and instead offer only reruns. If television was the only reward available, the child would likely be highly motivated to meet goals on Tuesday, but have much less incentive to work hard on Wednesday. However, the child may work hard both days if there would be good alternatives available on the list to reward positive behavior. A menu may also offer advantages for the parent as well; by listing a number of possible rewards, it is easier to "86" (as they say in restaurants when a menu item is out of stock) a reward that is not possible on a particular day (e.g., special time with Dad may not be available if he is out of town or working late on a particular evening; a trip to the park is not feasible on a rainy day).

A second consideration is to order and group the rewards on the list within a hierarchy. Let's be honest, if a goal is on the DRC, it is likely to be something that is challenging for the child to achieve. Therefore, it is reasonable to presume that even a single "yes" achieved on the DRC is an accomplishment for the child. Yet, most parents and teachers would say a day of mostly positive marks is better than a day of few positive marks. By placing the rewards in a hierarchy, children receive more desirable consequences for really positive days relative to so-so or challenging days. Still, the reinforcement for any earned goal is maintained and helps acknowledge the good things the child has achieved on any particular day. The hierarchy of rewards also sends a direct message to the child that perfection is not expected, and if things get off to a rough start, there is no reason to quit trying to meet daily goals.

Finally, *daily* is in the name *daily report card* for a reason. Most children would have difficulty delaying gratification for an entire week, and children who often require DRCs may have major difficulties in waiting for rewards. It is therefore important that initial intervention programs include daily feedback and daily rewards. Even though it may be easier to implement this program by providing rewards on a weekly basis, it is ill advised to begin the DRC program with such a lean reward schedule. (Most adults have a hard time waiting a week for a paycheck—one can only imagine what that length of time seems like to a child!)

Establishing a Reward Hierarchy

A hierarchical reward menu can be created through a number of approaches, and parents are encouraged to choose the approach that fits best with their parenting style and schedule. A simple way to create a hierarchical reward menu is to put all the rewards the child might like on a list and tell him or her to choose one reward for earning 40–60% of DRC goals, two rewards for 61–80% of DRC goals, and three rewards for 81–100% of DRC goals. Another approach includes grouping consequences by their reinforcing value. For instance, if a snack is desired but is not as important to the child as use of the computer, computer access might be reserved for exceptional DRCs (e.g., 81–100% of DRC goals reached), whereas a snack might be offered as a choice for an average day. A hierarchical menu can also be created by modifying the amount of time allotted at each reward level. To use the example of television time, 5 minutes might be awarded for every *yes* circled on the DRC for the day. This would ensure that more goals attained would result in increased levels of a desired privilege.

An alternative approach is to list a set of rewards and then begin to pair rewards together (e.g., television time and dessert). For each pair, the child should be asked which of the two rewards is preferred. After the first round, the preferred rewards could be paired up again, and the child could report on the preferred rewards from the second set. This strategy could be repeated until there was a small group of highly preferred rewards, and these could be the rewards emphasized on the DRC reward menu. This series of forced choices elicits the child's relative preferences, which may help to enhance the salience and reinforcing value of the DRC reward menu. Forced-choice approaches for rewards have been supported in the research literature (Cartwright & Cartwright, 1970), and there are materials available to facilitate these tasks with children (*http://cecp.air.org/fba/problembehavior3/appendixc.htm*).

Once a parent creates a hierarchical menu of home-based rewards, it should be viewed as a living document that is modified as the child's interests, the seasons, or the nature of the rewards change. There might be many reasons for modification—a child might complete all the stages within a favorite video game, making the video game less reinforcing and elevating the reinforcing value of another screen-based activity such as television. Further, trips to the park might not be any fun in blistering sun or freezing cold, causing this reward to be less applicable during certain times of the year. One-time rewards such as attendance at a special event or a special treat (going to the snack bar at an older brother's baseball game) might also be added or removed on an as-needed basis. The basic principle parents should keep in mind is that the reward menu should include enough variety and reinforcing potency to help the child maintain his or her motivation to meet goals on the DRC.

Common Pitfalls

It is clearly hard work to maintain a home-based reward system for a DRC. It is considerably more complex than just giving the child a reward. The reward system must be interwoven into the fabric of after-school activities, the parent must remember to provide the rewards, and the parent must monitor and manage access to awards contingent on the DRC results (e.g., if the child earned no television on a particular day, the parent must make sure the child is away from the room with the television when siblings may be watching it). Anyone who has tried to lose weight, quit smoking, or get more exercise also knows that it is very hard to maintain a new habit over long periods of time. All of these factors likely contribute to the difficulty of maintaining home reward programs, but they might also be informative when one thinks about the precipitators of common pitfalls.

The most common pitfall is inconsistency in the reward program. Between soccer practice, homework, getting held up at work, put-

---

CONSIDERATIONS IN SELECTING REWARDS

1. Is it a high-potency reward?
2. Is it an acceptable reward to the parent?
3. Is it feasible to provide?
4. Is it feasible to withhold?

ting dinner on the table, answering the phone, cleaning up, making lunches for the next day, walking the dog, taking care of younger and older children, and doing all the other things necessary to get through a day, it is no wonder parents have difficulty maintaining consistency. It is important to acknowledge all these competing demands at the outset of creating any reward program, and to encourage the parent to think about whether any rewards become less practical when viewed from this perspective. Educators and clinicians will find it helpful to think through the feasibility of potential rewards with parents, and even if one seems to be really rewarding to the child, if the parent feels that it would be difficult to maintain this reward over time, it is prudent to leave it off the list, at least until consistency can be ensured.

Another common pitfall is that for no apparent reason, rewards that were very important to the child at one time may fall out of favor. Parents should remain in tune with their child's interests and modify the reward menu as appropriate. An example of this relates to the fads that sometimes overtake schools. Sometimes a certain kind of trading card, apparel, or toy is strongly desired by a child, simply because the child's peers are all interested in that particular item. Over time, however, interest wanes as the peer group moves on to emphasize the next fad, or the child obtains the most desired tangibles, and what was once a highly valued item may now be cluttering the child's bedroom floor. The way to combat this possible pitfall is to stay attentive to the child's interests, watch what the child chooses to do when given free choice, and modify the reward list as needed.

Another challenge for maintaining the integrity of a home reward system is the presence of siblings, for multiple reasons. Siblings may undercut parental withholding of rewards. Imagine the above-mentioned household where a child did not earn television time, but siblings want to watch a program. Parents do not want to withhold the privilege from the siblings as well, which can create a difficult family dynamic or increase the monitoring demands placed on the parent. Parents often need to plan ahead to think about how they will withhold privileges in a way that does not punish other children in the home (or the parent him- or herself!).

There are some common pitfalls that parents *and* educators should be aware of when thinking about home-based consequences. One common issue is that the child may do something wrong that is not targeted on the DRC, such as fail a spelling test or shove another student at lunch. Often the impulse of the educator and parent is to withhold daily DRC privileges based on this new inappropriate behavior, even if the typical DRC goals are met. We advise against doing this because it undermines the intervention by sending the message that the goalposts can be moved at any time. Rather, this is a good time for the parent and teacher to touch base and determine whether this slip-up is a one-time event dealt with through alternative disciplinary procedures, one that should be carefully monitored, or one that warrants a modification to the DRC. In this way, if a target is added to the DRC, it is the product of the parent and teacher working in a proactive way, rather than a reactive way. It also gives the child an opportunity to make a positive choice and follow through by exhibiting the desired behavior.

Another all-too-common pitfall is that the child earned the reward for behavior related to the DRC, but the parent does not reward the child, as promised, for one reason or another. Sometimes a parent might be too busy, other times the parent might be irritated because of poor behavior at home, or sometimes the parent might not have a promised reward readily available (e.g., the parent has not gone shopping for the week and he or she is out of snacks). Regardless, these situations are all problematic because they introduce inconsistency into the DRC program. There are a number of ways to prevent this problem from happening, and most involve planning ahead by the parent. One major preventive approach includes the construction of the reward menu described previously; the use of the menu lets parents remove potential privileges or rewards that are unavailable while retaining others. Parents who understand the DRC principles will also quickly realize how it is important to provide the DRC rewards based on meeting the DRC goals, even if the child misbehaves in other settings. Taking away the rewards once earned would be like docking the pay someone earned for working Monday–Thursday because he called in sick on Friday. Most people would find this approach very unfair, and it is no different from the child's perspective. If a parent finds a child is only behaving when the DRC is in effect and then misbehaves once the reward is earned, strategies can be applied to modify this problematic situation (see Chapter 9).

A final consideration is that the reward menu might seem to be ineffective once implemented. In these cases it is important to revisit the steps that were used to put it together in the first place: Are the rewards rewarding? Is there a menu of rewards? Are they the best choices for the child? Parents should make sure that the child is not receiving reinforcement elsewhere. For instance, if the child is working on earning cell phone time but is able to go onto the computer and communicate with peers through social networking sites, it is unlikely that the reward will be a strong motivator. In this case, parents should work to incorporate all these social communication tools into the reward menu to maximize motivation toward meeting DRC goals.

A final set of comments relates to the role of educators in the home reward system. Although the rewards are provided at home, it is advisable for the parent to inform the teacher of those rewards. This is often done simply by sharing a copy of the reward menu with the teacher. This way the teacher can remind the child throughout the day of the potential payoff of meeting the goals on the DRC. In some of our cases that use a DRC, we also find that if the teacher is aware of the home-based reward plan, it may also help with consistency and follow-though by the parent. We recommend that the parent write what reward was provided on the DRC each day and return the DRC to the teacher for review. In this way, a communication loop is completed: The teacher sends the DRC home, the parent reviews the DRC, the parent provides consequences for the DRC, and the parent returns the DRC to the teacher (via the child) with the consequences noted. This communication between parent and teacher can go a long way toward making the DRC intervention a success, and it also promotes a collaborative and positive relationship between the parent and teacher with respect to the child's school-based behavior.

ESTABLISHING A SCHOOL-BASED REWARD SYSTEM

We have outlined above the procedures for constructing a home-based reward system for the DRC. Our approach is always to attempt to construct a home-based reward system for the DRC for the reasons outlined above. However, in some cases, for a variety of reasons, home-based rewards may not be practical, feasible, or consistently possible. In these cases, educators should establish a school-based reward system. It is important to underscore that the DRC intervention is unlikely to work efficaciously without a reward program in place in the home or in school, so it is critical that it is established in at least one of the two settings.

School rewards can be constructed in a manner similar to the approach to home-based rewards described above. There are some additional considerations required for the establishment of school-based rewards, however. First, many teachers balk at the idea of providing a special reward to one child when the other children in the class are not part of the reward system (especially if the other children are already consistently exhibiting the desired behavior!). It is advisable to think of rewards that are part of the school day. These might include recess time, access to the class computer, class jobs, hall passes, homework passes, and other activities that may be withheld following inappropriate behavior or incomplete work. These activities can then be made contingent on meeting DRC goals. An alternative approach is to permit the targeted child to choose a different classmate each day to participate in the rewarding activity. Rewards can also be administered in a separate location at the end of the day (e.g., a visit to the assistant principal's office or school counselor's office to play a brief game and receive encouragement/praise). A second consideration related to school-based rewards is similar to that outlined above for parents: Teachers have an incredible variety and number of responsibilities throughout the day, and remembering to administer school-based rewards may be difficult. It is important for the DRC coordinator to check in frequently with teachers regarding the reward program, and to problem-solve effective ways to support teachers in facilitating consistent implementation of rewards.

Some educators have found creative ways to promote consistent school-based reward programs. One of the challenges for teachers is providing a reward every day. A solution to this challenge is to use an approach that provides a reward less frequently, but that does not "water down" the child's experience in the program. An example of this is the Mystery Motivator program (Moore, Waguespack, Wickstrom, Witt, & Gaydon, 1994; Rhode, Jenson, & Reavis, 1992). In this program, a teacher draws a number of boxes on a sheet of paper (for the purpose of this example, let's say there are 10 boxes). In seven of the boxes the teacher might draw a smiley face, using an invisible ink pen. Each time the child is eligible for a reward, he or she should color in one of the boxes to reveal whether it has a smiley face or whether it is blank. If there is a smiley face, the child earns the reward, and if it is blank, the child is simply praised and encouraged to try to earn another opportunity to earn the reward. We saw these principles creatively applied in a preschool class where the teacher placed little slips of paper similarly marked within balloons. The child got to pop the balloon to reveal the slip (after a few observations, it was clear that it was a reward in and of itself for this particular child to stomp on the balloon to make it pop!). This approach, and ones like it, reduce the number of times a teacher has to provide a reward, and the random nature of the rewarding promotes the student's continued effort.

A final note on school-based rewards is that educators should be creative in thinking about these rewards. Similar to the home setting, there are many possible activities or items within schools for which access to them could be made contingent on behavior. In middle school settings, a child may be permitted to go to her locker 1 minute early if DRC goals are met. In elementary schools, jobs such as office messenger or passing out paper could be made contingent on a child's exhibiting appropriate behavior. One teacher we worked with really wanted a child to stay in his seat during her phonics lesson. If the child met this target, she designated him as her *Secret Messenger*. If the child earned the reward, the teacher brought him over to her desk and dramatically wrote a message and placed it in her envelope. She would then emphasize with the child that the message was very important and would he please deliver it to the principal with a friend of his choice. The child (and friend) then brought the envelope to the principal (who was working as a confederate with the teacher). He would open the envelope, read it seriously, and then thank the children for delivering such an important message. The attention from adults, opportunity to walk the halls, and the chance to choose a friend all served to make this simple interaction a powerful motivator for the child.

CHAPTER 7

Monitoring Progress
and Evaluating the DRC

The potential for the DRC to be useful as a tool both for intervention and for progress monitoring has been widely discussed in the research literature (e.g., Burke, Vannest, Davis, Davis, & Parker, 2009; Chafouleas, Christ, Riley-Tillman, Briesch, & Chanese, 2007; Evans & Youngstrom, 2006; Fabiano, Vujnovic, Naylor, Pariseau, & Robins, 2009a; Pelham, Fabiano, & Massetti, 2005). In this chapter we discuss the unique features of the DRC as a progress monitoring tool, and what we know about the technical characteristics of the DRC. In addition, we describe the process of evaluating response to DRC intervention using single-case design methodology. Finally, we provide detailed information about how to conduct a DRC Evaluation Interview, wherein data collected over the course of intervention are used to make decisions as to whether the intervention has been effective and how best to proceed.

DRCs AS PROGRESS MONITORING MEASURES

One of the first conceptualizations of the DRC as both an intervention strategy and progress monitoring measure was provided by Pelham (1993), who noted the utility of the DRC both as an intervention and as a tool to assess functional impairment as part of a comprehensive assessment of treatment response for students with ADHD. It has been asserted that the focus of assessment in progress monitoring should be placed on areas of specific impairment as opposed to the symptoms of disorders such as ADHD (Pelham, Fabiano, & Massetti, et al., 2005). That is, although there may be overlap in the domains of impairment and symptoms of emotional and behavior disorders, it has been argued that once a diagnosis has been reached, the more logical assessment targets are areas of functional impairment. These are more likely to represent malleable behaviors targeted for treatment. The DRC items in this book represent a fairly comprehensive pool of treatment targets and indicators of functional impairment. In other words, these items represent the problems typically experienced by children with emotional and behavior problems in the school setting that impact their academic and social functioning.

It has been argued that, in addition to these indicators of impairment, measures designed to assess more general behavior problems (e.g., attention problems, oppositional behavior, social withdrawal) can be a useful element of a comprehensive assessment system for evaluating treatment response. Assessing both domains affords measurement of short-term performance objectives in addition to the more global impact of intervention over time (Volpe, Briesch, & Chafouleas, 2010; Volpe & Gadow, 2010). When used in intervention, DRCs are dynamic in that items can be dropped from the DRC once goals are consistently achieved and often new items added. To the extent that DRCs change over time and differ from one case to the next, they are not well suited well for long-term progress monitoring and cannot be used to make normative comparisons. Generally speaking, if the forms change over time and differ among students, comparisons cannot be made across time and persons, respectively. Needed are general outcome measures for social behavior analogous to those found in formative academic assessment (e.g., oral reading fluency). To date, no approach to general outcome measurement for social behavior has been widely adopted, but different approaches are beginning to emerge (see Chafouleas, Volpe, Gresham, & Cook, 2010, for a special issue on emerging trends in behavioral assessment).

Over the past decade there has been an increase in research studies investigating the psychometric characteristics of the DRC when used as an intervention (e.g., Fabiano et al., 2009a; Pelham et al., 2002; Pelham, Fabiano, & Massetti, 2005) or solely as a formative measure of student classroom behavior (e.g., Chafouleas, Riley-Tillman, Sassau, LaFrance, & Patwa, 2007). As we discussed in Chapter 4, a number of different formats to DRC have been studied. These formats have included Likert-type scales (e.g., Chafouleas, 2011), goal attainment scaling (Burke et al., 2009; Vannest et al., in press), and the yes–no format that we have advocated in this book (e.g., Fabiano et al., 2007; Pelham, 1993). All of these approaches would fall under a broader class of assessment instruments now commonly referred to as *direct behavior rating* (DBR), a term that was first coined by Chafouleas, Christ, and colleagues in 2007 to describe an array of measures that combines aspects of both systematic direct observation and behavior rating scales. As the term implies, DBR (which would include DRC) is a direct form of assessment in that the forms are completed by raters immediately after a specified period of observation. Typically, observation periods for DBR are short (e.g., several minutes or several hours) as compared with typical rating scales that are designed to summarize informant experiences with a target student over weeks or months. Like rating scales, however, items are rated on some kind of scale. Numerous authors have discussed the potential advantages of DBR, including feasibility and flexibility, over other progress monitoring methods (e.g., Briesch & Volpe, 2007; Chafouleas, Christ, et al., 2007). The fact that these measures typically are quite short (between one and five items) and can be completed by teachers in the naturalistic environment lends to their feasibility. These measures are considered quite flexible in that the items comprising the measures can be individualized for each student (e.g., Fabiano et al., 2010; Volpe & Gadow, 2010). Further, the DRC as a measure compares favorably to lengthier and costlier measures such as objective classroom observations (e.g., Fabiano et al., 2009a).

Over the past decade Sandra Chafouleas, T. Chris Riley-Tillman, and their colleagues have published over 25 studies investigating the psychometric characteristics of the Likert-type-scale approach to DBR, wherein the informant is asked to rate student behavior on a scale indicating the proportion of time the student exhibited the behavior of interest. This work has focused on a single-item approach to DBR, wherein each broad construct is measured by a single item. After investigating a small group of items, this group has increasingly focused on three single-item scales (Academically Engaged, Respectful, and Disruptive). This research group has programmatically studied various aspects of DBR methodology, including the optimal number of gradients on a scale (e.g., Chafouleas, Christ, & Riley-Tillman, 2009), the length of observation sessions (Riley-Tillman, Christ, Chafouleas, Boice-Mallach, & Briesch, 2011), the wording of items (e.g., Christ, Riley-Tillman, Chafouleas, & Jaffery, 2011), and the effects of training on the accuracy of ratings (e.g., Schlientz, Riley-Tillman, Briesch, Walcott, & Chafouleas, 2009). In addition, they have investigated various sources of error, including rater, occasions, and setting (Chafouleas, Christ, et al., 2007; Chafouleas, Briesch, et al., 2010); the acceptability and use of the method (e.g., Riley-Tillman, Chafouleas, Briesch, & Eckert, 2008); and the sensitivity of the scales to changes in student behavior in response to classroom interventions (Chafouleas, Sanetti, Kilgus, & Maggin, 2012). Indeed, the knowledge base on this approach to DBR has become extensive and is encouraging (see Chafouleas, 2011; Christ & Boice, 2009). To our knowledge, the Likert-type-scale approach, which has been the focus of these studies, has not been employed in a DRC intervention, but has been employed as general outcome measures to evaluate DRC intervention (Chafouleas et al., 2012). Much more information on single-item DBR can be found at *www.directbehaviorratings.com*.

Goal attainment scaling is another approach to scaling items for DRC. In this approach specific target behaviors (e.g., completing tasks, remaining in assigned area) are identified and anchor points are written for each of 5–7 points on a scale. The process of establishing anchors for each scale begins by establishing the first three anchor points representing the bottom, middle, and top of the scale. These anchors should describe the typical level of behavior (representing a problem), behavior that might be exhibited when the student is having a good day, and behavior representative of long-term goal attainment, respectively. Once these anchors have been established, intermediate anchors in each direction can be written. Specific examples of these scales can be found online at *www.edbrc.tamu.edu*. Less is known about the psychometric characteristics of this approach, compared to the other two approaches discussed here, though several studies examining the reliability of teacher-rated forms are encouraging (Burke et al., 2009; Vannest et al., in press).

Like the goal attainment scaling approach to DRC, the yes–no scale approach has employed items that represent specific targets for treatment (see the DRC Item Table). Although one could think of each item on such a DRC as representing a single-item scale for that particular target behavior (e.g., "Starts work with fewer than three reminders"), in evaluating the psychometric characteristics of this approach, the group of items selected for a student are thought to comprise a multi-item scale (e.g., Pelham et al., 2001). This makes sense since, in the context of evaluating short-term treatment response, it can be argued that the construct of interest is not some generic measure of symptomatology (e.g., ADHD, oppositional behavior), but rather each student's unique pattern of functional impairment (Volpe, Briesch, & Gadow, 2011). Pelham, Fabiano, et al. (2005) summarized studies investigating the technical characteristics of DRC using the yes–no format. They reported acceptable internal consistency (alphas between .77 and .88). The ranges of temporal stability reported by Pelham, Fabiano, et al. (2005) were somewhat low (between .57 and .62), but recently much higher estimates have been reported (Fabiano et al., 2009a). Arguably, one of the most important considerations is the extent to which teachers can accurately rate behavior, given the many other demands on their attention during instruction. Correlations with observational measures have been moderate to large (between .43 and 1.0). Moderate to large correlations (IO = .58–.74; OD = .51–.72) with the IOWA Conners (Loney & Milich, 1982), demonstrate the degree of overlap between measures of functional impairment and relevant symptomatology. Also important to users of the DRC is the degree to which it is able to measure changes in behavior that result from intervention. Indeed, scales using the yes–no format have been found sensitive to the effects of both pharmacological (e.g., Pelham et al., 2001, 2002) and behavioral treatment (Pelham, Massetti, et al., 2005; see also Fabiano et al., 2007). Taken together, these studies support the use of the yes–no format DRC for use in measuring short-term intervention effects.

We have provided a very brief synopsis of the literature concerning the technical characteristics of the DRC as progress monitoring measures. Although the overwhelming majority of research attention, on both the single-item Likert-type approach, and the goal attainment scaling approach has focused on their use as progress monitoring measures outside of the context of DRC intervention, theoretically either could be used to format a DRC for purposes of intervention if one were to establish goal attainment criteria for each item. However, of these two, goal attainment scaling seems to be the more appropriate format for DRC intervention because the anchors are potentially more meaningful for students. Nevertheless, we favor the yes–no scaling approach, because in our experience, both teachers and students find the format easy to follow. The focus for students clearly lies in whether they meet a goal or not. For teachers, it may be easier to keep track of whether goals are met as opposed to paying close attention to the frequency or duration of a behavior after it is clear that a goal has been met or not. Moreover, this approach has been used most consistently for the purpose of intervention.

GENERAL CONSIDERATIONS FOR CHARTING PROGRESS MONITORING DATA

In Chapter 3 we discussed several different approaches to charting baseline data, which are useful for several purposes: the selection of DRC items, the goals to be included in items, and the settings in which the DRC forms will be used. We explained how the spreadsheet we have made available to those who purchase this book can be used to store and summarize data in these different formats. The last of the formats we discussed involves converting raw data collected during baseline (e.g., number of inappropriate noises during each interval) into the percent of possible points the target student would have earned had a specific goal been established. This is the format we use to monitor student progress over the course of intervention, since once the DRC has been established, teachers no longer need to record raw frequencies or percentages, but instead they record whether each goal was met during each interval (the yes–no format). That is, using single-case designs, or for that matter, anytime we want to make comparisons across time, it is necessary that our measurement is consistent across those occasions.

We have created another spreadsheet for progress monitoring (available for purachsers to download at *www.guilford.com/volpe-forms*) for use in entering and charting progress monitoring data. To use the spreadsheet, the user enters the labels for each DRC item, the settings in which they are to be used, and the number of settings observed on a typical day. Filling in this information creates a form on a separate sheet in the Excel workbook where progress monitoring data are entered. On that sheet the user enters the number of points the student has earned (yeses) for each DRC item for each day of intervention. Corresponding to each of these cells is a cell to indicate the number points that have been earned for that DRC item for that day. These cells are automatically populated by the value the user entered to indicate the points possible on a typical day. If for some reason, fewer points are possible on a particular day, the user can modify the relevant cell. If there was no opportunity for a student to earn points for a specific DRC item (e.g., no homework due on Monday), the user can enter *NA* in the "points earned" column, and the "points possible" column will automatically be populated with an *NA*. These data will be ignored in all calculations. Entering these data will automatically create a time series chart for the total percentage of points earned for each day of intervention. In addition, the percentage of points earned for each DRC item will be charted separately. Space is provided to enter baseline data so that an A-B design (discussed later in this chapter) is charted for each DRC item and for the total percentage of possible points earned.

INTERPRETING SINGLE-CASE DATA

We do not intend to provide a detailed discussion of single-case designs here, as to do so easily could fill a complete volume. Indeed, there are many current sources of information on single-case designs in the literature (e.g., Cooper et al., 2007; Kazdin, 2010; Johnson & Pennypacker, 1993), with one in particular in this book series (Riley-Tillman & Burns, 2009). Nevertheless, often single-case design methodology is discussed outside of the context of a particular application. Specific applied examples often are used for the purpose of conveying concepts, but these may not be directly relevant to the particular application the reader has in mind.

In this chapter, we have the unique opportunity to discuss single-case designs with particular application to the DRC in mind. Before we begin to discuss specific designs, however, it may be helpful to walk you through some of the basics of baseline logic. We understand that for many readers this will be a review. *Baseline logic* is a method of reasoning wherein we apply the three elements of prediction, verification, and replication to draw a conclusion as to whether our intervention has been successful (Cooper et al., 2007). We use our case study of Sky as an example of how we might apply this logic to determine if our DRC intervention has been working.

In Figure 7.1 we have summarized Sky's baseline data for the total points she would have earned for each of the 5 days of baseline data collection if we had applied her DRC goals to those data. Remember that these data were collected as raw frequencies, and we later applied the goals to calculate the baseline data for progress monitoring purposes. The spreadsheet we created for baseline data makes these calculations for us. We talked about the many ways baseline data can be useful. The utility of baseline data in our discussion here is that they establish a point of departure by which to gauge the effectiveness of our intervention. In our example, the baseline data represent the level of Sky's behavior (as it relates to the targets of DRC intervention) under "business-as-usual" conditions.

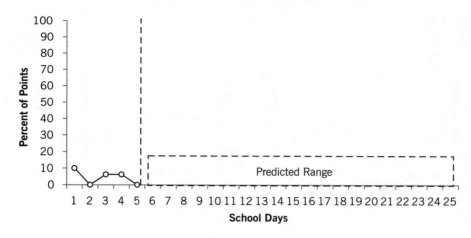

FIGURE 7.1. Prediction based on Sky's baseline data.

These data tell us much about how things are going for Sky in the classroom relative to the goals we have set for her. First, the percent of points she would have earned over the baseline period is low—lower than 15% of points each day. Moreover, there is relatively little variability in Sky's performance across the 5 days (between 0 and 10%). To the right of baseline data in Figure 7.1 we have indicated (with a dashed rectangle) the range of values we might expect if we did nothing different. That is, if we continued to collect these data without initiating the DRC intervention, we might *predict* that the data would follow the same pattern. In the context of a DRC intervention (where increases in the percent of points earned is desired), if data collected during intervention were to fall consistently above the dashed rectangle, as in Figure 7.2, we might apply the following logic:

1. If the intervention is effective, the data will increase with the introduction of the intervention.
2. The data did increase with the introduction of intervention.
3. The intervention is effective.

Although data such as that summarized in Figure 7.2 often are used in applied settings to demonstrate that an intervention has been successful, such a case is based solely on prediction and is an example of a logical fallacy called "affirming the consequent." The invalidity of this form of reasoning can be made clear by the following example:

1. If it is raining, the grass is wet.
2. The grass is wet.
3. Therefore, it is raining.

Just as there are many reasons why the grass might be wet (e.g., sprinkler, morning dew), there are many explanations for why a change in Sky's behavior might occur at a certain point

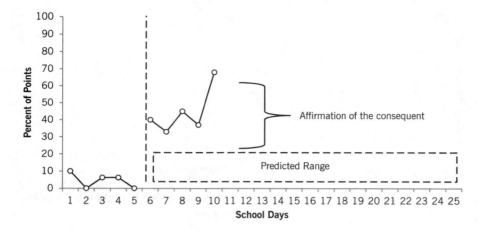

FIGURE 7.2. Affirmation of the consequent.

in time. Some might be more obvious to the consultant (e.g., change in classroom teacher), than others, and of course sometimes behavior changes without any perceptible reason.

In Figure 7.2 affirming the consequent is straightforward because there is a clear separation between the predicted range and the actual level of the data in the intervention phase. In Figure 7.3 we have charted the same values for intervention data, but charted baseline data with an ascending trend. You can see the effect on our prediction and how this would influence any inferences we might make about the intervention. There is no doubt that Sky's behavior was getting better; that has not changed between the two examples. What has changed is our ability to take the first step in suggesting that the intervention was responsible for the improvement.

Another type of undesirable baseline data would be data that are highly variable, as in Figure 7.4. When data look like this, they typically suggest that there is something influencing the student's behavior for which we have not accounted. Ideally, we would like to see if we

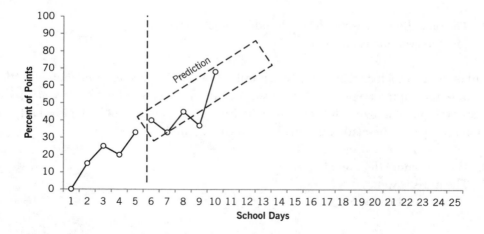

FIGURE 7.3. Ascending baseline data.

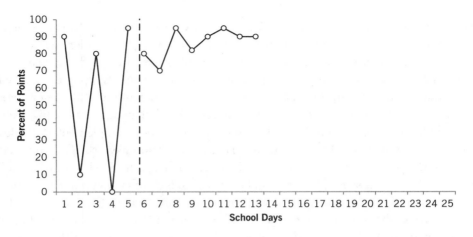

FIGURE 7.4. Variable baseline data.

might isolate the influence of that factor to obtain more stable data, since our range of prediction spans almost the entire range of possible values. The more likely course of action for someone working in an applied setting is to press on with the intervention (e.g., Sidman, 1960, as cited in Cooper, Heron, & Heward, 2007) and hope that the intervention data increase in level with a corresponding decrease in variability, as in the intervention phase of Figure 7.4.

From our discussion, it is clear that when charting the percent of points earned in the evaluation of DRC intervention, there are two types of desirable baseline data: (1) stable data with a flat trend, and (2) stable data with a descending trend. So, we have talked about how we can take the first step in making the case for an effective intervention by affirming the consequent. The examples we have provided above, wherein we charted both the baseline and intervention data, are typically referred to as case studies or A-B designs, wherein *A* represents the baseline phase, the *B* represents the intervention condition (e.g., DRC intervention), and the vertical dashed line indicates the change from one phase to the other.

It is clear to most of us that the most common design utilized in school settings is the B design, where a teacher makes a referral and the consultant gets to work immediately with the intervention without first collecting baseline data (cf. Riley-Tillman & Burns, 2009). We have designed the procedures in this book to facilitate the use of at least an A-B design in evaluating the effects of DRC intervention, by building the collection of baseline data into the DRC design process. Although this is an improvement over a B design, we already have talked about the logical fallacy on which it rests. With relatively minor changes to intervention procedures, one can significantly strengthen the defensibility of the single-case design employed to evaluate the effectiveness of the DRC intervention. Let us talk first about what is missing from the A-B design. We have discussed the element of baseline logic referred to as *prediction*, but in talking about A-B designs, verification and replication do not apply.

Let's say that we have been successfully administering a DRC intervention with Sky, and we think that the intervention would work well for another student in the building who has just been referred to us. Say we show the data from Figure 7.2 to the teacher as evidence that the intervention works very well. "Wait a second," the teacher says. "How do you know this student's behavior did not just change on its own?" You think to yourself, *ah, a student of inductive reasoning to be sure.* What would convince this teacher, or any critical consumer, that it was indeed the intervention that caused the behavior change and not something else? One way to attempt to answer that question is to temporarily remove the intervention. Using prediction again, we would assume that the improvements in Sky's behavior would continue if the intervention was left in place. If we discontinued the intervention, and Sky's behavior returned to baseline levels, we might be more convinced that if the intervention was never implemented, the level and trend of baseline data would have continued. That is, we would have *verified* our prediction. Say we showed the data in Figure 7.5 to the skeptical teacher instead. This is an example of an A-B-A design. The teacher might say that to be truly convinced that you did not just measure a "flash in the pan," he or she would have to see you do it again. That is, the teacher would like to see a *replication* of the measured intervention effect (affirmation of the consequent). In Figure 7.6 we present an A-B-A-B design. The A-B-A-B or reversal design (Baer, Wolf, & Risley, 1968) is generally the most powerful single-case design for demonstrating functional relationships between an intervention (environment) and behavior—that is, in determining that an intervention was responsible for a measured change in behavior (Cooper et al., 2007). As you can see from Figure 7.6, the reversal design includes all the elements of an A-B-A design, but adds a replication of the affirmation of the consequent. A reversal design makes quite a convincing case for the effectiveness of an intervention when the interventionist can demonstrate behavior change in a predictable and repeatable fashion.

As a school-based professional, much of this discussion likely strikes you as academic because teachers and parents are reluctant (for obvious reasons) to withdraw an apparently effective intervention. Likewise, in some cases it would be unethical to remove an effective intervention as in the case of self-injurious or physically aggressive behaviors (Baer et al., 1968). In other cases, behaviors may not be reversible; indeed we often hope they will not be so. One obvious example is the case of academic interventions. That is, we would not expect a student to suddenly forget basic math facts learned as part of an academic intervention.

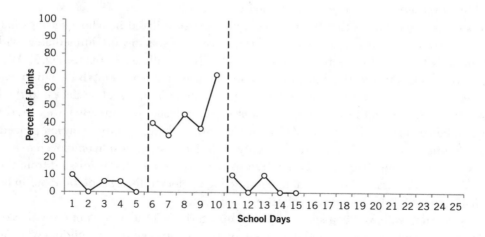

FIGURE 7.5. Example of an A-B-A design.

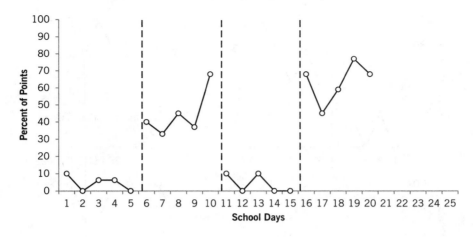

FIGURE 7.6. Example of an A-B-A-B design.

A multiple-baseline design (MBD) is an alternative to reversal designs that allow the application of prediction, verification, and replication without having to withdraw an intervention. At least in terms of published reports, it is the most common single-case design used to evaluate interventions in schools and other applied settings (Cooper et al., 2007). In an MBD, baseline data are collected for several responses and the intervention is applied sequentially across them. There are three types of MBD: (1) MBD across behaviors, (2) MBD across settings, and (3) MBD across subjects. Let us look at MBD across behaviors as an example for how we might evaluate our DRC intervention for Sky. We have designed a DRC for Sky consisting of four items, assessed in each of four settings, and an additional item for homework completion that is assessed one time daily. To simplify, we have selected three items for Sky and demonstrate how they might be evaluated in an MBD across behaviors (i.e., across DRC items). In Figure 7.7 you can see that we have collected baseline data for each of the three items (Fewer than two instances of inappropriate talking, Starts work with fewer than three reminders, Talks back fewer than two times). We can use the same procedure for charting data that we discussed in the previous chapter. That is, for each DRC item we would chart the percentage of points earned each day. To stagger the implementation of intervention for the MBD, we would provide feedback to the student and parents (along with the home-based rewards) incrementally. That is, once we have established stable baseline data, we would provide feedback on only the first item (inappropriate talking). The transition from no-feedback (baseline) to feedback (intervention) is indicated by the dotted horizontal line. Notice that while we are in the intervention phase for the first data series, we continue to collect baseline data for the other DRC items. Once we have affirmed the consequent for the first DRC item, we can introduce the intervention for the next item and so on.

In Figure 7.7 you can see that we have three A-B designs in our MBD, with progressively longer baselines as we look down the list of DRC items. The elements of prediction and affirmation of the consequent are much the same as they were in our earlier discussion of A-B designs. For verification, however, we must make comparisons across data series. Remember that we

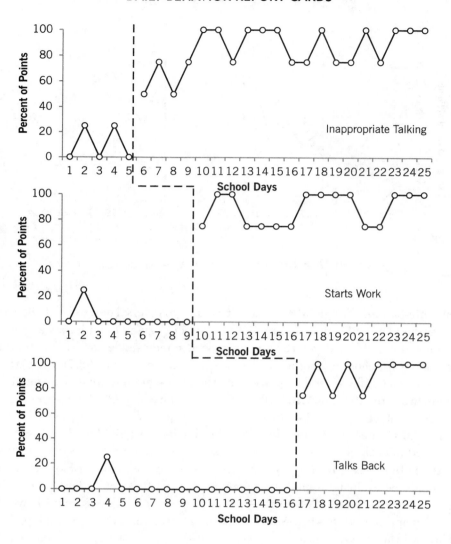

FIGURE 7.7. Multiple-baseline design across behaviors for Sky.

demonstrated verification in our A-B-A design example when we removed the intervention and the behavior returned to baseline levels. There we verified that if we did nothing, the behavior would have persisted as it did during the baseline phase. In an MBD we do not remove an intervention, but the staggered implementation of feedback allows us to compare baselines in the second and third data series (*starts work, talks back*) to the data series above them (*inappropriate talking* and *starts work*, respectively) to examine the question of verification. Specifically, look at data points 6–9 in the *starts work* data series. Notice that they remain at zero, even after feedback was introduced for *inappropriate talking*. There we have verified that if we did nothing, Sky's behavior would have remained at baseline levels. We can do the same thing for points 10–16 for *talks back* (comparing against *starts work*). Notice in this design that we also have replicated the effect of intervention we found for *inappropriate talking* for both *starts work* and *talks back.* Using an MBD across behaviors in the context of a DRC is a fairly straightforward process. It simply means that feedback on some behaviors is withheld temporarily in order to demonstrate experimental control using baseline logic. Although this might all seem a bit egg-headed, there are practical advantages to staggering the introduction of feedback across DRC items. Although this method has not been evaluated empirically, it would seem that providing feedback to the student one item at a time could help the student adjust to the intervention.

You might already be thinking about how you could use an MBD across *settings* instead. Using Sky as an example again, we could use a composite of points (summing points for each DRC item) and compare them across settings. The chart for this example would look very similar to that in Figure 7.7, but instead of each data series representing a different DRC item, we would have four data series, each representing a different setting where the intervention is in place (i.e., reading, writing, math, and science). We could first implement the intervention in reading, and then add writing, and so on. Finally, if you wanted to implement the intervention with multiple students, you could employ an MBD across subjects (students). Here each data series would represent a different student.

One additional point to consider is that, over the course of intervention, items may be dropped from the DRC, new items added, and goals for individual items can be changed. Any change in the DRC should be reflected on the chart for that student's progress. In Figure 7.8 we have documented a change we might have made to Sky's DRC. Specifically, for the *inappropriate noises* item, we changed the criterion from eight to five.

Although there are more detailed sources of information concerning single-case design (e.g., Kazdin, 2010; Riley-Tillman & Burns, 2009), we thought it would be useful to review basic design components and address specific applications to the DRC before moving on to the process of conducting a DRC Evaluation Interview. In the next section we review the procedures for conducting this interview with parents and teachers.

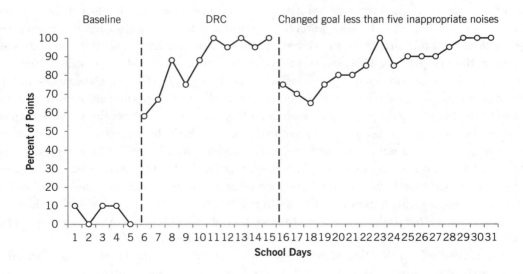

FIGURE 7.8. Documentation of change in DRC procedure.

THE DRC EVALUATION INTERVIEW

The objectives of the DRC Design Evaluation are (1) to determine the extent to which the goals of the DRC intervention have been met; (2) to decide what changes to the intervention plan, if any, are necessary; and (3) to plan for next steps. In Appendix J we have included a form to help you structure the DRC Evaluation Interview. It includes a list of items that should be brought to the interview.

With regard to goals for the DRC intervention, we can think about goals established for each item and also the overall percentage of DRC goals met by the student each day. Looking at Sky's DRC (see Figure 1.1), we see that some goals may represent actual long-term goals for the particular behavior targeted by the item in question. The item "Completes assignments within allotted time" is an example of such an item. Clearly, if Sky consistently meets this goal, it is easy to ascertain that the long-term goal has been reached. Other items, however, may be adjusted over time, as in the example we used for inappropriate noises. The long-term goal for the item was established in the DRC Design Interview. That goal was established at fewer than

> ### OBJECTIVES OF THE DRC EVALUATION INTERVIEW
>
> 1. **Determine the extent to which the goals of the DRC intervention have been met.**
> 2. **Decide what changes, if any, are necessary to the intervention plan.**
> 3. **Plan for next steps.**

two instances of inappropriate noises. These long-term goals are necessary to establish whether the DRC intervention has been successful. Decisions with regard to goal attainment fall under three possible categories: (1) the student has not made progress toward the goal (e.g., essentially no change in behavior from baseline), (2) the student is making progress toward the goal, and (3) the student has reached the goal (see Kratochwill & Bergan, 1990).

If the student has made no progress toward the goal, it is important to determine whether the intervention has been implemented with integrity and to assess to what extent the intervention was acceptable to stakeholders (parent[s] or guardians, teacher[s], student). In Chapter 9 we list problems that may arise over the course of intervention and how they might be addressed. Assessing the integrity of a DRC intervention can be a straightforward process since each step creates a paper trail, otherwise known as *permanent products*. That is, the teacher ratings, parent or guardian signatures, and notes on the DRC all create a permanent record by which to assess treatment integrity. We have included other materials in Appendix I, the Treatment Integrity Form, that you can use to assess the degree to which the intervention was delivered as planned. To take advantage of this benefit, a procedure must be established to preserve the DRCs so that they are not misplaced. This is no small task, as DRCs can often get lost when being transported from home to school, and vice versa. Of course, points awarded to the student can be made contingent on the student's handing in the DRC to the teacher, which would offer a powerful incentive for students to ensure the integrity of record keeping. Also, as we mentioned in Chapter 4, it can be advisable to use carbon paper to create a copy of daily ratings.

If it is determined that the intervention was delivered as planned and still was not effective, it can be discontinued. It is likely that the student requires a more intensive intervention. If treatment integrity was low, steps might be taken to address the factors that led to low integrity in a revised intervention plan. If these issues cannot be addressed, then, again, the intervention should be discontinued. If the student is making good progress toward reaching long-term goals, then the intervention should remain in place. The DRC Evaluation Interview is a good time to review criteria for individual DRC items and otherwise discuss ways the intervention could be further enhanced (e.g., revisiting reward menu, troubleshooting any integrity issues). If the student has reached the long-term goals established during the DRC Design Interview, then one possibility is to keep the intervention in place, and slowly increase the time between home-based rewards. In Chapter 4 we talked about the possibility of students earning both daily and weekly rewards, but the latency between occasions wherein the student may earn these rewards can be systematically increased. Another possibility is teaching the student to monitor and manage his or her own behavior through a self-management intervention. The following chapter is devoted exclusively to that topic. Transitioning from a DRC to a self-monitored DRC (SM-DRC) can be a relatively straightforward process since much of the intervention already is in place.

CHAPTER 8

Incorporating Self-Monitoring within the DRC Intervention to Promote Maintenance and Generalization

Amy M. Briesch and Brian Daniels

Over the course of this book it has hopefully become clear that the DRC is not only an effective and feasible intervention for improving the classroom behavior of children and adolescents, but also an incredibly flexible intervention as well. The DRC can be constructed in order to address a wide range of behaviors (e.g., peer relations, disruptive behavior) and can be implemented across a variety of settings (e.g., classroom, playground) at a frequency that is deemed appropriate for the particular student (e.g., end of class period, end of day). One element of DRC construction and implementation that has remained constant throughout the past several chapters, however, has been the role of the student in intervention procedures. That is, adults (i.e.,

Amy M. Briesch, PhD, is Assistant Professor in the School Psychology Program in the Bouvé College of Health Sciences at Northeastern University. Her research interests involve the identification and integration of feasible social behavior assessment approaches into school systems; the use of self-management as an intervention strategy for reducing problem behaviors in the classroom; and the role of student involvement in intervention design and implementation. She has authored over 20 peer-reviewed journal articles to date related to these research interests.

Brian Daniels, MS, CAGS, is a certified school psychologist and an alumnus of the Specialist School Psychology Program at Northeastern University. He is currently enrolled in the Doctoral School Psychology Program at Northeastern University. His research focuses on the implementation of feasible and efficient behavioral interventions, such as DRCs and the use of self-management, to increase students' academic engagement and reduce problem behaviors in general education settings. Prior to returning to full-time graduate study, Mr. Daniels worked as a school psychologist in Massachusetts, where he helped his school district transition to a response-to-intervention (RTI) system for providing and evaluating behavioral interventions for students.

teachers, parents) have maintained primary responsibility for the design and implementation of the intervention.

Although we inevitably associate the term *report card* with some sort of external assessment, there is no magic rule that mandates that only teachers can wield the power of the red pen. Once the student has become familiar with the DRC procedures and has demonstrated behavioral success with the intervention, the next logical step toward promoting maintenance and generalization is to add a self-rating component. Within a self-monitored DRC (SM-DRC) approach, the student is charged with self-assessing his or her behavior and comparing it to an external standard or goal. The feedback is therefore self-generated, rather than being generated externally by teachers and parents. As adults, we engage in this type of personal goal setting and self-evaluation on a regular basis, and it is exactly this type of behavior that allows us to accomplish tasks independently. When we want to lose 10 pounds before the summer or finish a novel before the next book club meeting, we set reasonable goals for ourselves (e.g., lose 1 pound a week for the next 2 months, read 10 pages a day for the next 3 weeks) and then regularly reassess our progress toward these goals to determine whether we need to make adjustments to our behavior. This feedback loop was described by Kanfer (1970) as involving three phases: (1) assessing one's own behavior, (2) comparing that behavior to a goal, and (3) using the information gained through this comparison to make necessary adjustments to future behavior. When we see, at the end of the week, that we were supposed to have read 70 pages, but are only on page 20, we may substantially increase the amount of time set aside for reading at the end of the day in order to increase the likelihood of meeting that long-term goal. Students can also be taught these self-regulatory strategies by having them complete the SM-DRC.

There are several advantages inherent in incorporating self-monitoring into a DRC intervention. First, by teaching the student how to carry out procedures, the intervention becomes instantly transportable. Once the student has mastered procedures in one classroom, the intervention can be extended to other classroom periods (e.g., within a secondary school context) or even nonclassroom settings (e.g., hallways, recess), thereby promoting generalization of the target behavior(s). Second, implementing an SM-DRC may help to promote long-term maintenance of behavior, given that the student is taught lifelong self-regulatory skills. Finally, because responsibility for conducting ratings is gradually shifted to the student, it may be more feasible for the classroom teacher to implement the DRC with multiple students.

WHAT DOES THE SM-DRC LOOK LIKE?

All of this may make sense philosophically, but the million-dollar question at this point is what modifications are needed in order to incorporate self-monitoring into a traditional DRC intervention? Ideally, minimal changes will be needed to the existing procedures so that the transition can be made quickly and easily. Given that the target behaviors have already been identified, the goals established, and progress monitoring has been ongoing, much of the "heavy lifting" has already been done! The steps that remain (i.e., creating the SM-DRC, training the student, conducting self-ratings, providing feedback) are outlined below.

THE SETUP: GETTING READY TO RATE

Creating the Card

Transitioning from the DRC to the SM-DRC requires only minor modifications designed to maximize usability for students. First, because some students may need more explicit reminders about what the target behaviors look like, examples and non-examples can be listed directly on the SM-DRC for the student's reference. It is best to select no more than three examples in order to avoid what we call "card clutter." The best examples are those behaviors that occur with some regularity or for which there may be some ambiguity in interpretation. A great way to involve students in the development of the SM-DRC is to help them to brainstorm which specific examples should be included on the card. Let's take the item "Fewer than two instances of inappropriate talking" as an example. The student could be asked first to provide examples of what appropriate talking looks like in the classroom (e.g., waiting to be called on before talking, talking to neighbors about group project). Once these positive examples have been listed, the student could then be asked to think of some examples of when he or she has talked at inappropriate times (e.g., calling out before being called on during math). If the teacher knows that there are some behaviors for which interpretation may be more ambiguous (e.g., whispering to neighbor), it is a good idea to also list these behaviors on the card.

Second, in modifying the DRC, the goal is to make the card appropriate for the student's developmental level and sufficiently personalized. The language used in the operational definitions and examples should be easily understood by the student; for younger children, for example, pictures of desirable behaviors can be used in place of text. In addition, student interest in the intervention can be strengthened by asking him or her to help design the actual card. The student's interests (e.g., race cars, kittens) can be incorporated through clip art or simply by printing the DRC on paper that is the student's favorite color. Particularly when working with younger children, we have found that even these small ways of personalizing the SM-DRC can go a long way toward promoting student investment!

Finally, in order to minimize materials for the student to manage, we recommend adding a data collection box to the actual SM-DRC. As mentioned in Chapter 3, most of the DRC items assess frequency of occurrence (e.g., "Talks back fewer than two times") or the presence/absence of a behavior (e.g., "Keeps hands and feet to self"). As such, the student can use tally marks in the data collection box to indicate each time that a behavior occurs (e.g., talks back, touches others) or the number of reminders needed to perform a given behavior (e.g., put away materials). The student can then use these raw data to evaluate whether or not a particular goal was met (see Figure 8.1 for an example). Given the increased complexity associated with determining proportional behaviors (e.g., percentage of compliance), we recommend sticking to frequency-based items within the SM-DRC (e.g., "Starts work with fewer than two reminders").

Training the Student

Although the student will already be familiar with the behaviors being rated, a training session should be scheduled between the teacher and student prior to beginning the SM-DRC intervention phase (see Appendix K for an SM-DRC Training Form). The first goal of this meeting should be to review the items and ensure that they are in student-friendly terms that are con-

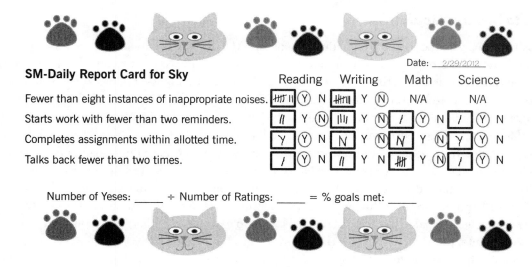

FIGURE 8.1. Example of an SM-DRC for Sky.

sistent with the student's developmental level. Older students may easily understand behaviors such as "teases peers" or "appropriately asks an adult for help when needed"; however, younger students may require more concrete definitions of target behaviors such as "makes fun of class-mates" or "raises hand when I need help." Good SM-DRC items are those that a student can look at and instantly know whether he or she is performing the behavior.

A second goal of this meeting should be to demonstrate and practice the actual rating procedures. Once the definitions have been reviewed, the student can be given the actual DRC and asked to rate the items as the teacher acts out both examples and non-examples of the target behavior(s). These role plays should be used not only to ensure that the student understands the procedures (e.g., when to make ratings, where to place tally marks), but to check for understanding of the behaviors being rated as well.

In addition to helping the student identify and operationally define target behaviors, the teacher should also use the meeting to discuss the rationale for incorporating the self-monitoring component. The SM-DRC intervention allows the student to take control of his or her behavior, and, in our experience, we have found that a main selling point for students to use this self-monitoring tool is to reduce nagging from their teachers and parents! In general, the meeting between the teacher and student should be collaborative and include as much input from the student as possible to ensure that student investment is maximized.

> **STUDENT SM-DRC TRAINING TASKS**
>
> 1. **Review items and ensure that language is student-friendly.**
> 2. **Brainstorm examples and non-examples of target behavior(s).**
> 3. **Demonstrate and practice rating procedures.**
> 4. **Discuss rationale for self-monitoring component.**
> 5. **Establish procedures for data collection.**

Establishing Goals

As previously stated, one of the main goals of an SM-DRC intervention is to increase the student's awareness of his or her own behavior. To accomplish this, the teacher should first take some time to review data that have been collected to date, highlighting improvements in behavior that were noted as the student began the DRC intervention. This is a great opportunity to engage the student in a conversation about the ways in which the intervention has positively influenced his or her performance in school and to celebrate the successes experienced to date. At this point, the teacher may also work with the student to revisit the DRC goals and determine whether any changes are warranted. That is, in moving to incorporate self-monitoring into the DRC intervention, it is expected that students have been successful in earning the majority of possible points up until this point. In the beginning, it may be most straightforward to use the same overall goal (e.g., 80% of DRC goals met to earn reward) that was in place during the previous intervention phase. Over time, however, as the student consistently experiences success with the self-monitoring component, the ante can be raised by making the criterion more challenging (e.g., meeting 100% of goals).

THE EXECUTION: RATING BEHAVIOR AND PROVIDING FEEDBACK

Once the goals have been set and the SM-DRC created, it is time to begin implementation.

Conducting the Ratings

As discussed in Chapter 5, it is helpful to have a brief face-to-face meeting with the student to review goals at the beginning of the rating period. For some students, it may be helpful to place the DRC on top of the desk, where it can serve as a visual reminder of behavioral expectations. If this makes the student self-conscious or draws unnecessary attention from classmates, however, the SM-DRC can be placed inside of the student's desk or in a notebook/binder. In either case, it is important that the card be easily accessible so that the student can quickly pull it out to record any necessary instances of behavior.

Providing Feedback

Within a traditional DRC intervention approach, teachers are encouraged to check in with students to provide feedback and encouragement toward their goals; however, parents are charged with central responsibility for reviewing ratings and assessing whether goals were met. Within a SM-DRC approach, however, greater emphasis is placed on the teacher–student meetings as a way to monitor the integrity (i.e., did the student actually complete the ratings?) and accuracy (i.e., did the student conduct a realistic self-assessment?) of student ratings. Ideally, these meetings should occur in close proximity to the DRC ratings so that the student's behavior is still fresh in both the student's and teacher's minds.

SM-Daily Report Card for Sky		Reading	Writing	Math	Science

Date: ___2/29/2012___

Figure content:

Fewer than eight instances of inappropriate noises. — Reading: ⊞⊞ II (Y) N — Writing: ⊞⊞III Y (N) — Math: N/A — Science: N/A

Starts work with fewer than two reminders. — Reading: II Y (N) — Writing: IIII Y (N) — Math: I (Y) N — Science: I (Y) N

Completes assignments within allotted time. — Reading: Y (Y) N — Writing: N Y (N) — Math: N (N) Y — Science: (N) Y (Y) N

Talks back fewer than two times. — Reading: I (Y) N — Writing: II Y N — Math: ⊞ Y (N) — Science: I (Y) N

Number of Yeses: __7__ ÷ Number of Ratings: __14__ = % goals met: __50%__

FIGURE 8.2. Example of a teacher-completed SM-DRC.

During this meeting, the student would bring his or her ratings and work to her teacher to calculate an overall percentage of goals met (i.e., number of "yeses"/number of ratings; see Figure 8.2 for an example). The primary role of the teacher in this meeting is then to facilitate a brief, but targeted, discussion centered on the student's behavior. If the student was successful in meeting many or all of his or her goals, it is important for the teacher to provide positive feedback and encouragement. If he or she was not successful, however, the student may be asked to identify which specific behaviors prevented him or her from meeting the goal and to problem-solve what could be done differently next time.

Collecting Outcome Data

Although the student is responsible for completing ratings throughout the SM-DRC intervention period, we recommend that rewards continue to be linked to teacher ratings during this new phase. The reason for this choice is concern about rating accuracy that accompanies most types of self-reports (particularly when there are rewards attached to them!). When the SM-DRC component is first introduced, the teacher should continue to complete the DRC according to the rating schedule that has been in place since baseline. Although the earning of rewards should be based on the teacher's ratings (i.e., were a sufficient number of goals met?), it may be useful in the early stages of self-monitoring to offer an extra incentive for rating accuracy in order to calibrate the student's ratings. As such, the student and teacher would independently complete the DRC and then calculate a percentage of agreement across their ratings (i.e., number of agreements/total number of ratings; see Figure 8.3 for an example). The student could then earn either a bonus point or an extra privilege if a sufficient level of rating accuracy (e.g., 80%) were achieved.

Once the consultant and teacher believe that the student is completing the ratings accurately and with fidelity, teacher ratings can be conducted less frequently. The teacher may first cut back to one rating period per day and then continue to fade ratings until they are only conducted once or twice a week. An example of such a data collection schedule can be seen in Figure 8.4.

FIGURE 8.3. Example of SM-DRC for Sky with student and teacher agreement.

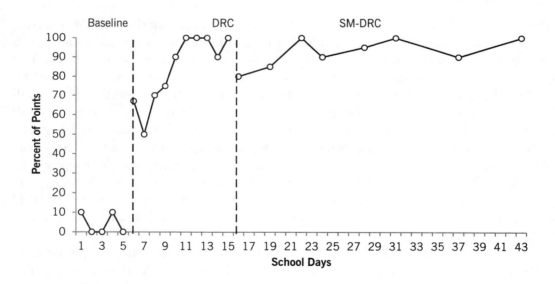

FIGURE 8.4. Example of teacher-collected data during an SM-DRC period.

Home–School Communication and Incorporating Rewards

The final piece of the puzzle involves establishing a system of home–school communication as well as an appropriate reward system. We refer the reader back to Chapters 5 and 6 for specific guidelines, but note that there are several ways in which communication and rewards can be structured. One possibility may be to review student ratings intermittently with the teacher during the day, but then have the parents calculate the total number of points earned and provide home-based rewards if applicable. As an alternative, both the review of ratings and administration of rewards can occur in the school setting. Regardless of where the rewards come from, it is important that information about the student's behavior be communicated to both school and home to help foster a positive home–school collaboration and to ensure that the student feels supported from all sides.

CHAPTER 9

Problems and Solutions

Behavioral interventions can be hard work, and those who have implemented them know that there are a number of potential problems that can arise. The intent of this chapter is to review some of the common pitfalls that may be encountered by parents, teachers, or students. As we discuss them, we also introduce potential solutions. It is our expectation that at least some problems will arise throughout the process of establishing and implementing a DRC—in fact, if a facilitator of a DRC intervention hears of no problems at all, it may be wise to check in to see how the program is going—because the absence of problems is an unusual outcome following the initiation of any intervention!

SCREENING

• **Problem.** From time to time a student with significant classroom-based impairments may not be identified as in need of support on a full-class screening. Sometimes this error occurs because the problem is narrow in scope, sometimes it occurs because the teacher underestimates the extent of the problem, and sometimes the reason is not clear.

• **Solutions.** If a teacher reports impairment in a functional domain impacting learning or the student's social interactions with others, even if a student is not identified on a screen, there is justification in pursuing intervention. Some students may benefit from relatively simple DRCs that target only a behavior or two, or a single time of day (e.g., cafeteria behavior; language arts work completion). It may be good practice to simply ask teachers whether they have any behavioral concerns for any additional students beyond those identified through a screening (see Chapter 2) when providing feedback from the screening assessment. This question would provide an opportunity to check whether the screening was comprehensive in identifying appropriate cases for intervention.

Also, at times, teachers may underestimate the extent to which a student requires a DRC intervention, sometimes because a teacher has grown accustomed to problematic behaviors, sometimes because the teacher has accommodated such behaviors (e.g., no longer requires the student to complete entire assignments), or at other times may be because the teacher has a high tolerance for behaviors most teachers would find problematic. In these cases, consultants might use alternative sources of evidence beyond the screening (e.g., curriculum-based measures; discipline referrals) to support the documentation of the need for additional intervention.

- **Problem.** More problems are reported by the teacher as being problematic for an individual student during the initial meeting than those picked up on the screen.

- **Solutions.** Consultants would do well to consider the screening as a launching point for their interactions with the teacher. The screening likely represents a good start for further assessment that can occur using the Problem Identification Interview Form, Appendix C (or other tools) to better quantify the nature, severity, pervasiveness, and intensity of problematic behaviors exhibited by a target student. Consultants and teachers should both understand that student behavior can change rapidly, and that what was a problem one day may resolve soon thereafter. By the same token, new problems may arise unexpectedly. To deal with this unpredictability, the DRC should be conceptualized as a "living document" that is readily adapted and modified based on the student's present needs.

- **Problem.** Too many kids are identified through screening, making individual DRCs difficult to implement.

- **Solutions.** A screening may at times identify a *classwide* problem rather than an *individual* behavior problem. In these cases, consultants might decide to utilize a classwide DRC intervention or an alternative intervention based upon principles similar to those of the DRC (e.g., good behavior game, group contingency, classwide point or token system). Studies have investigated classwide applications of the DRC and found that a DRC, consisting of one or two items, leads to rapid improvements in disruptive and academic behaviors in general education classrooms (e.g., Dougherty & Dougherty, 1977; see also Lahey et al., 1977). Saudargas, Madsen, and Scott (1977) investigated the classwide use of a single general item (work completion) and studied how students responded to having feedback on this item sent home once a week (fixed interval) compared to having the feedback go home each day for a random selection of students (variable interval). The only stipulation in the randomization was that each student had to have feedback sent home at least once per week. In this condition the students did not know which day a report would be sent home. Of interest, the variable condition was the most effective and the most favored by teachers. Together, these studies suggest that an optimal approach for classwide DRC intervention may be to select one or two general items and to rate them on a random selection of students (with each student getting feedback sent home at least once a week).

The advantage of a classwide program is that it may be easier for the teacher to implement and maintain. In contrast, multiple individual DRCs would be more cumbersome for most teachers. Once a good classwide program is in place, and the teacher has benefited from general behavioral control, it may be appropriate to revisit the need for individual DRCs for any students who are still exhibiting problematic levels of behavioral challenges.

PROBLEM IDENTIFICATION

- • **Problem.** Teachers report too many problems.

- • **Solutions.** It is important to convey to teachers that, in essence, "Rome was not built in a day." If a teacher identifies a large number of problems to be addressed on the DRC, it is the consultant's job to help the teacher pare down the list to the key behaviors that will be initially addressed. As a rule of thumb, no more than three to five behaviors should be targeted at any one time. Multiple approaches might be effective in helping teachers reduce the number of targets initially identified. One approach is to rank-order behaviors that are the most severe/problematic at the top, down to the behaviors that are the least problematic, as in the ISIS procedure described in Chapter 2. The DRC might begin by targeting those behaviors that the teacher believes are the most important; additional behaviors can be addressed once the initial ones are under control. An alternative approach would be to base the target behavior selection on a good functional assessment. For instance, a teacher might identify work completion, out-of-seat behavior, teasing, and off-task behavior as problems that need to be addressed. A functional assessment of these problematic behaviors might suggest that the latter three behaviors are avoidant in nature, and that they are all exhibited by the student in an effort to escape the demands of completing academic work. If academic work completion with accuracy was targeted on the DRC, this may actually address all the behavioral concerns; that is, the student could not engage in those other problematic behaviors because they are incompatible with completing seatwork accurately.

- • **Problem.** Teachers report too few problems.

- • **Solutions.** It is generally not a problem if teachers have only a few problems that they want to address with a particular student, but there can be consequences of too few targets on the DRC. One consequence is that by identifying only a single target or two on the DRC, a student is placed in an "all-or-nothing" situation. This can be ill-advised, especially for a child with a low-frustration threshold or one who has low self-confidence in his or her abilities to meet the targets. This is because a single "no" on the DRC results in a disproportionately negative message relative to a DRC with more targets. One solution for this situation is to include some additional targets, even if they are not proximally problematic, to add some "cushion" to the child's DRC. Although the targets may not need to be addressed urgently, they may serve to improve the usefulness of the DRC intervention for the target or two that do require the intervention.

In some cases, if there is only a single goal for the DRC, alternative interventions might also be considered. These might include using high-frequency behaviors (e.g., playing a preferred game) to reward low-frequency behaviors (e.g., completing assignments) (Premack, 1959; Cooper et al., 2007), classwide contingencies (e.g., "If the class has fewer than five instances of tattling today, we will take a nature walk outside"), or punishments (e.g., "Any instance of aggression will result in an office referral"). In these cases a DRC is not needed.

DRC CONSTRUCTION

- **Problem.** One "no" for a really severe behavior is washed out by lots of "yeses" for minor behaviors.

- **Solutions.** We discussed above the problem of a single item having a disproportionate impact on the child's ability to earn a reward. Well, the opposite can also occur. Adults may feel chagrinned at the prospect of praising a child for earning "yeses" for remembering homework materials when it has the effect of canceling out a "no" for a more serious behavior (e.g., punching another student). There are a number of ways to address this problem. One solution may be to take out some of the less important targets, at least for a little while. A very savvy teacher once wanted to make "No aggressive behaviors" a very prominent target on the DRC. In this case she typed the target out five times in a row—and she circled five "yeses" if the child was not aggressive. This had the effect of weighting the DRC toward this goal and encouraged the child to pay extra attention to progress toward this goal. An alternative strategy might be to establish special home- or school-based rewards that are linked to success on the target that is being emphasized. That is, earning a particularly high-ranked reward can be made contingent on the item of interest. Although such steps add to the complexity of procedures, the changes are relatively minor and well justified for certain problem behaviors or areas that represent a particular challenge for students.

- **Problem.** It is difficult to maintain coverage across teachers/classes.

- **Solutions.** Sometimes we may want to target student behavior in places other than the home classroom. These settings might include the school bus, bus line, hallway, cafeteria, specials classes, or the after- or before-school program. If problem behavior is occurring in these settings, the DRC may be a great way to address them. A simple way to offset problems in these settings is to ensure that someone communicates with the adult in charge, explains the DRC, addresses any questions, and creates a plan for implementation and accountability. Beyond that, because the child may be in these settings irregularly (e.g., physical education classes may only occur once a week) or different adults may be in charge on different days (e.g., in the cafeteria), it may be important to identify a point person (e.g., counselor, homeroom teacher, school psychologist) to work to maintain consistency over time.

The problem becomes more pronounced when a student moves to middle school and multiple teachers are the rule rather than the exception. Some solutions to this issue again involve communication—between teachers, students, parents, and the teaching team. In these situations, it is generally advisable to have one point person in charge of ensuring the integrity of the entire program. It is also helpful if the middle school student has the DRC in an easily accessible place. In many cases this might be a binder or agenda that the student brings to each class. The goals can be written in the day's calendar or printed on a label that is affixed to the bottom of it. As the teachers in each class check to see that the homework is written down correctly, they can also quickly provide an accounting of the student's behavior on DRC targets. Integrating the DRC into necessary material for all the classes also reduces the chances that the student will misplace or forget it (same goes for the teachers!).

WORKING WITH STUDENTS

- **Problem.** The student opposes the DRC program/doesn't bring it home/loses it.

- **Solutions.** Most students are not oppositional toward the DRC if it is presented in a positive way and the possibility to earn rewards is emphasized. A negative response might suggest that the child misunderstands the program, or the introduction to the DRC did not convey a positive valence. Revisiting the introduction and focusing on these aspects of the discussion might solve the problem.

POINTS OF VIEW TO CONSIDER WHEN TACKLING A PROBLEM RELATED TO THE DRC

1. **Teacher**
2. **Parent**
3. **Child**
4. **Classmates**
5. **Others supporting the DRC**
6. **Some combination of 1–5**

In other cases, a child may simply be oppositional to any new demand or program, the DRC being no different. In these cases it is important for adults to stay the course, highlight successes, and consistently implement the reward and privilege system based on behavior. It is also important to ignore any complaints/arguments regarding the program and simply implement it as intended. When the right combination of rewards is chosen, most children eventually "get with" the program.

- **Problem.** The student can't keep track of where he or she stands in meeting goals.

- **Solutions.** To solve this problem, a good assessment of the problematic behavior should be conducted. Sometimes a child does not have the cognitive ability to monitor standing toward goals (i.e., due to developmental level, working memory). In these cases a concrete metric for meeting goals should be constructed (e.g., tally marks on the board, removing marbles from a jar for each target behavior exhibited). This approach will help the child keep track of his or her standing in relation to meeting goals.

In other cases the teacher may not be clearly conveying feedback related to DRC progress. Teachers should directly and specifically label rule violations or behaviors that are related to the DRC goals in a consistent manner so that the child can tune in to the feedback and understand where he or she stands with respect to meeting the goals.

- **Problem.** The student does not understand what you are asking him or her to do.

- **Solutions.** Some of the same solutions noted above might apply here. In addition, teachers can utilize role plays and describe examples and counterexamples to help the child understand the behaviors that are being targeted. Praising specific behaviors that are incompatible with the target behavior may also be helpful. Further, clearly labeling the target behavior when exhibited will help the child understand what is triggering the teacher's negative feedback.

Another solution could be to teach the child a replacement behavior. We recently worked with a young child who hit others any time a child came into her personal space. The teacher took this child aside and taught her to say "no thank you" when another child came too close. (The teacher also told the class that if a student says "no thank you," the person asking needs to find another activity.) The student had a target added to her DRC to use her words to inform the other child that she did not want him or her to be so close to her. The student began using the alternative, socially appropriate behavior almost immediately, and the rate of aggression noticeably dropped.

- **Problem.** The student behaves very negatively after exceeding goal threshold and missing the target.

- **Solutions.** Sometimes you just can't win. A child may work really hard to meet goals on the DRC, but due to a low frustration threshold, the child may behave even *worse* if the goals are not met. The thought process here is that "I'm not going to earn the reward anyway, so I might as well get my money's worth." An initial solution to this issue is to ensure that the student has a range of rewards available on a menu, as mentioned in Chapter 6. This range will encourage the maintenance of appropriate behavior, even if a goal or two is missed.

At times, however, this approach will not be enough. If the intervention team determines that the child is behaving negatively when realizing that he or she has surpassed the threshold for the goal, a solution is to keep the child guessing about what the criteria for meeting a goal are. This can be done by leaving the goal criterion blank (e.g., "Interrupts _____ or fewer times"). The teacher then gets a paper bag and puts slips of paper in it that say "0," "1," "2," and so on. Wisely, there should be more slips that say "0" and "1" than larger numbers. Children like to have a slip or two in the bag that state "free pass." Then, when it comes time to evaluate the DRC, the child draws a slip out of the bag and that becomes the criterion the child needed to meet in order to get a "yes" on the DRC. This approach improves behavior in two ways. First. it prevents the child from having an opportunity to "melt down" during an activity where a goal is not reached. Second, it promotes excellent behavior because the child quickly learns that he or she might draw a "0" from the bag, and a smart approach is to behave very well so as to meet the goal if that number happens to be drawn.

WORKING WITH PARENTS

- **Problem.** Parent does not attend the initial meeting.

- **Solutions.** It is important to acknowledge that the school schedule does not often align well with the schedule of many families. Although it is easy to assign negative attributions to parents who fail to attend at a parent meeting, it is always possible that a parent is dealing with a bigger issue than school problems (e.g., sick or dying family member; stressful work or financial issues; his or her own psychopathology). Nevertheless, teachers must work with the child in spite of the parent's inability to participate. For these cases teachers may rely more heavily on school-based rewards; however, it is important to continue to send the DRC home each day to maintain communication and feedback with the parent.

It may also be possible to promote parent participation by removing the expectation that a parent needs to be physically present at a school meeting. With technologies including conference calls, Skype, and e-mail, parents and teachers can often communicate quite effectively without the parent even stepping foot in the building. Keeping parents updated on the decisions made and interventions established at each step in the process can also help ensure effective communication. It is good practice to assume that the parent *wants* to be involved in the process, even if there are no outward signs to support this assumption. At the least, if the parent is continually informed of the process, he or she can't come back and complain about the lack of effort or of being kept out of the loop!

THE CASE OF THOMAS

Throughout this book we have described the case of Sky, a child who is supported through the use of a DRC. As educators know, every child they work with will be a little different, so below we outline another case—that of Thomas (the case is based on the authors' clinical work, but key details have been modified). This case is intended to illustrate how the DRC can be implemented in a middle or high school setting with a team approach.

Thomas is a seventh-grade middle school student . He is a bright boy, routinely earning B's across his report cards. His teachers agree that he is capable of A-level grades, but his average is often undermined by projects or homework assignments that are submitted late or not at all. He is well known to the school psychologist, principal, and assistant principal in the middle school, as he is often referred to the office due to problematic behavior. The most common causes of office referrals include verbally abusing teachers and other adults in the school, teasing peers, and being actively noncompliant. It was recently discovered that Thomas was one of three children in the cafeteria who bullied another student so often that she began going to the nurse's office with a stomachache at lunchtime to avoid the cafeteria incidents. Thomas's school counselor used to work in the elementary school, and she remembers him being in trouble frequently while in school there as well. Currently, there is an acrimonious relationship between the school and Thomas's mother. She has been upset because she feels he is being singled out, and she does not feel that the school is providing appropriate supports.

Thomas's middle school does not have a screening system such as those described in Chapter 2. Thomas was referred to the child study team in the school because of continued disruptive and problematic social and academic behaviors. The team decided that a DRC might be a potential solution, and the school psychologist met with the child's team of teachers to initiate the intervention. The teaching team was readily able to generate a list of potential target behaviors (i.e., "Be prepared for class with completed homework"; "No instances of verbal disrespect"; "Needs no more than one warning for noncompliance").

However, it was clear right away that there were some barriers to implementing a DRC. The teaching team thought it was strange to suggest that Thomas should receive a reward for doing the things all the other kids routinely do without rewards. The team also seemed skeptical that there would be sufficient time to evaluate Thomas's performance. A few teachers chuckled to themselves when the school psychologist suggested that Thomas would be responsible for bringing the DRC to them to sign at the end of each class. Things really began to go downhill when the school psychologist began to explore who should work with Thomas's mother to create a home-based reward system. One teacher shook his head and said, "There's no way that will work."

The school psychologist carefully noted each of these problems, and she started working through them. She began by asking the teachers what they were currently doing to monitor and deal with Thomas's behavior. Generally, the teachers reported that they would sometimes ignore him, sometimes remove him from class via an office referral, and other times repeatedly correct him within the classroom. When asked, they all reported that they felt their current approach was ineffective. "That being the case, what do we have to lose by trying this? Would it be worth a try, even for a few weeks at the start?" the school psychologist asked.

At the end of this meeting, the school psychologist decided to take a break with the teachers and contact Thomas's mother next. Although she was aware of a longstanding history of conflict between the parent and the school, she had no history of interactions with this parent. It took 2 days, phone calls to different numbers, and a trip to the emergency contact file to locate an e-mail, but the school psychologist finally reached Thomas's mother. She introduced the DRC like this:

> "I imagine you are not happy with how this school year has started, and I am sure out of everyone involved you are the one most concerned with what is best for your son. I am concerned that currently school is a very negative place for Thomas. He has been getting frequent negative feedback about his behavior, and this is not effective. I am sure you are tired of receiving negative feedback as well. I want to propose to you a different type of approach . . . it is called a *daily report card*. Each morning I will meet with Thomas, greet him with a positive attitude as he starts his school day, and I will review all the expectations for the day with him. If you'd like, I can also check to see that he's organized with his completed homework ready to turn in. Then, each day, his teachers will let him know after class how he did with regard to meeting expectations. He'll bring this checklist home to you each day after school for both of you to review, and here's where you come in. In this program, we find it always works best if parents can provide a positive consequence at home for meeting goals and expectations on the daily report card. I am not talking about big, expensive prizes; these should be activities or possessions Thomas currently has as a right that you can take away and award back as a privilege for having a good day at school. Would you be willing to discuss with me a plan for a set of home-based rewards?"

Thomas's mother agreed, and she was able to construct a home-based reward menu that used screen-time (video games, computer, television, tablet) as a contingent privilege. Armed with this information, the school psychologist again met with the teaching team. The team was generally impressed that Thomas's mother had agreed to the program, although a few teachers reserved a healthy skepticism. Yet, all were more willing to explore the DRC intervention during this second meeting. The goals were kept the same as the ones identified in the first meeting, and one teacher suggested that Thomas have the DRC targets printed in his agenda, which he brought to every class. She reported checking it at the end of class to ensure homework was written down correctly anyway. She did not think it would be too much trouble to evaluate three additional behavioral targets at the same time. Most of the other teachers agreed to use the same procedure, with the exception of Mr. Carruthers, Thomas's social studies teacher. He thought there was no way he would have time at the end of class to fill out the book, given that he usually had six to seven students come up to his desk with questions. In his case, he agreed to e-mail the school psychologist if Thomas received a "no" on any goal—otherwise the presumption should be that the goals were met.

The school psychologist prepared the DRC in Thomas's agenda, called the parent to review the goals established and discuss the reward system one final time, and started the program. The school psychologist also set up a second meeting with Thomas at the end of the day for 1–2 minutes. The purpose of this meeting was to review the DRC, provide encouragement for goals met, provide an opportunity to call/meet with teachers who forgot to complete the DRC, and ensure Thomas had all the materials he needed for homework that evening. Although the school psychologist anticipated that the program would require some modifications, and she planned to follow up with teachers and the parent to ensure that the components of the intervention were being implemented with integrity, the initial DRC intervention was a good start.

- **Problem.** The parent does not consistently reward the DRC.

- **Solutions.** This is a common complaint from teachers and, in our clinical experience, the largest stumbling block to getting teacher buy-in for a DRC program. There are often two reasons for this problem: either the parent never rewarded the DRC, or the parent initially rewarded but the consistency of the home-based rewards has decreased. We discuss solutions for both of these problems.

If the main problem is that the parent has never initiated the home reward system, a straightforward solution is to create a school-based reward program. Class jobs, free time, computer time, homework passes, lunch in the classroom, and other class activities all are potential school-based rewards. Although sometimes not as potent as rewards that might be offered in the home setting, school-based rewards are a viable alternative. An additional advantage of school-based rewards is that they are more immediate than home-based rewards and may therefore better support students who are very impulsive or have difficulties with delaying gratification until after school.

If a parent initially rewarded the DRC consistently but has "fallen off the wagon" of late, it is a good idea to contact him or her and share the observations of the child's recent behavior. As noted in Chapter 6, it is expected that the reward menu will change over time, and sometimes it is necessary to remind parents of this point. It is also suggested that part of the initiation of the DRC program includes writing a space on the bottom of the form for the parent to sign each night and note the reward provided. This way teachers can see how consistent the home-based rewarding approach is and attempt to remediate short-term inconsistency before it becomes more pronounced. At times school-based rewards can be initiated to off-set temporary parental inconsistency as well (e.g., change in parental work schedule will require a modification of rewards).

WORKING WITH TEACHERS

- **Problem.** Teacher stops the DRC program after a short period of implementation.

- **Solutions.** It is not uncommon for teachers to discontinue interventions after only a few days of implementation. Martens and Ardoin (2002) reported that the modal number of days teachers implement a consultant's recommendations is zero! Anyone beginning a DRC intervention with a teacher should be cognizant of this basic reality and plan for it ahead of time. Sometimes it is helpful to think about and discuss potential barriers to effective implementation ahead of time with a teacher. For instance, if a teacher says that there is not enough time to review the DRC with a child each morning, perhaps a counselor or classroom aide could take over this responsibility. If a teacher forgets to evaluate the DRC, empowering the child to ask for feedback at each designated interval (and this is likely to happen if the child is motivated by the reward system) can resolve the problem. Another important consideration is that a clearly operationalized intervention plan, including unambiguous designations of who is responsible for what, can help alleviate problems of diffusion of responsibility, points where there is a lack of clarity, and it promotes accountability (see Appendix G).

IMPLEMENTATION

- **Problem.** The child is not being successful on the DRC.

- **Solutions.** There are a number of reasons a child may not be successful on the DRC. These include the possibility that the child, parent, or teacher does not understand the intervention or how it works, the behavioral criteria are too hard for the child to reach, the rewards are not motivating or not administered consistently, the teacher is not appropriately monitoring or providing feedback on the target behaviors, or the child may simply be incapable of performing the targeted behavior (e.g., a child with a learning disability may have difficulty with completing reading assignments targeted on the DRC).

The solutions to this problem are likely to be as numerous as the potential reasons for the problem. Most solutions will include a careful functional assessment of the problem and an investigation of the contributors. Regardless of the reason, it is imperative to attempt to determine a path that promotes the child's success on the DRC. This might include modifying targets, making criteria for meeting targets more liberal, or adding targets that the child may be more likely to meet in the short term.

- **Problem.** The child always obtains all yeses.

- **Solutions.** This can be a good problem to have if the child is behaving appropriately and has no impairment in the classroom! Rarely, however, is this the reason why a teacher or parent may find this situation to be a problem. There are a few qualifications before addressing this problem. First, it is important to ensure that the teacher is monitoring and providing feedback on the DRC effectively and appropriately. Further, it is worth discussing whether some target behaviors are no longer issues, and should be removed, and whether new behaviors should be targeted instead.

Once there is a clear idea of the context in which the child is receiving "all yeses," the goal for all involved should be to calibrate the DRC so that the child is earning approximately 70–80% of yeses each day. This could be accomplished with no change in criteria at all—the teacher could simply enforce the DRC more consistently. This can also be accomplished by making the criteria for meeting a target more restrictive. Finally, targets can be added and removed to better calibrate the DRC to make it appropriately challenging for the child. In many cases, some combination of these tactics may be needed to solve this problem.

- **Problem.** The student does not like receiving feedback on behavior.

- **Solutions.** Some children, especially those in middle or high school, may dislike receiving behavioral feedback from the teacher, whether it is positive or negative. These situations run the risk of the child acting out on purpose to avoid teacher feedback throughout the class.

In these cases, teachers might set up signals or other feedback mechanisms with the child ahead of time to prevent the need for verbal feedback throughout the class. Teachers could also withhold feedback until the end of class or until a certain threshold is met (e.g., two interruptions have occurred and three during the class period will result in missing the goal). Other procedures that incorporate feedback that may be reserved for private interactions with the student include interventions such as check and connect (U.S. Department of Education, Institute of Education Sciences, What Works Clearinghouse, 2006).

SELF-MONITORING

- **Problem.** The student has not consistently completed the self-ratings using the DRC.

- **Solutions.** It is possible that the student did not have the materials necessary to conduct self-ratings. Make sure all necessary materials (i.e., SM-DRC, writing utensil) are available to the student. It is helpful to have spare copies of the SM-DRC available in case the student loses it. Sufficient prompts to monitor and record behavior may not have been provided to the student. Be sure intermittent verbal (e.g., "Don't forget to use your DRC") or nonverbal (e.g., tapping the card or desk) prompts are provided to the student. It also may be possible that the student is not sufficiently motivated to complete self-ratings. Determine whether rewards continue to be sufficiently reinforcing and help the student to select new rewards if necessary. It may also be beneficial to have the student complete a forced-choice reinforcement survey to identify which functional category of reinforcement (e.g., positive social reinforcement, tangible reinforcement, removal of unpleasant stimuli) he or she most desires. It may be that the intervention procedures draw unwanted attention to the target student. In such cases, efforts should be made to make intervention materials and procedures more discrete. For example, the DRC may be made smaller or kept in the student's folder.

In this chapter we have attempted to offer solutions to the obstacles most likely to stand in the way of efficiently implementing the procedures we have outlined in this book. No doubt you will likely face obstacles not addressed here. We hope that we have communicated that the DRC is a decidedly flexible approach to managing student classroom behavior. Although we have attempted to break down the steps involved in implementing the DRC into manageable components, only you the end user will know how best to modify the procedures in your own setting and for the individual cases with which you will work.

Appendices

ISIS Teacher Rating Form

Teacher: _____   School: _____

Date: _____   Grade: _____

Directions: This form can be used to rate students' behavior that interferes with their learning or the learning of others. In the long columns on the right, please list the names of the five students in your classroom whose behavior is of greatest concern to you in this regard.

For each item below, indicate your level of concern regarding each student using the following scale:

1 = Slight concern
2 = Moderate concern
3 = Strong concern

Leave the space blank if the student does not exhibit the behavior or if the behavior is not a concern for that student.

	Student Name	Student Name	Student Name	Student Name	Student Name
1. Does not complete classwork on time					
2. Inaccurate or incomplete classwork					
3. Does not start assignments independently					
4. Writes illegibly					
5. Missing or incomplete homework					
6. Does not turn in class assignments					
7. Does not correct own work					
8. Fails to pack needed materials for home					
9. Transitions poorly between activities					
10. Argues with teacher					
11. Disrespectful to adults					
12. Loses temper					
13. Does not ask for help/asks for help inappropriately					
14. Noncompliant					
15. Disrupts others					

(continued)

16. Does not follow directions					
17. Calls out					
18. Moves around the room					
19. Uses materials inappropriately					
20. Uses inappropriate language					
21. Tattles on other children					
22. Destroys property					
23. Has conflicts with peers					
24. Mumbles or speaks incoherently					
25. Argues with peers					
26. Bossy					
27. Nosey					
28. Does not participate in group activities					
29. Distracted by others' negative behaviors					
30. Does not work well with others					
31. Teases					
32. Makes irrelevant comments					
33. Comes to class unprepared					
34. Unorganized					
35. Does not put away belongings					
36. Takes too long when using bathroom or water fountain					
37. Asks to leave classroom frequently					
38. Makes self-deprecating comments					
39. Cries, complains, whines					
40. Does not participate in class					
41. Leaves room without permission					
42. Bumps, hits, or kicks others					
43. Does not respect others' personal space					
44.					
45.					
Total Rating					

Screening Interview Form

Teacher(s): _____ Date: _____

School: _____

Prior to meeting with the teacher, identify the student with the largest total rating and write his or her rating and name in the space next to Rank "1." Continue to rank the students in descending order of total rating.

Interview Tasks

1. Examine rankings from the ITRF and make adjustments based on the magnitude of teacher concern.
2. Assess the fit of the DRC for each student.
3. Organize follow-up tasks.
4. Establish prioritized list of students.
5. Schedule Problem Identification Interview.

1. Student Ranking

Discuss with the teacher whether the rankings below match the level of teacher concern.

Rank	Total Rating	Student	Fit	Priority
1				
2				
3				
4				
5				

AA = additional assessment, FP = follow up with parent, SBR = school-based reinforcement, IP = internalizing problems.

2. Assessment of Fit

Assess fit of intervention for the student and his or her parent.

3. Follow-Up Tasks

Use form on next page to assign any follow-up tasks.

4. Establish Priorities

Based on teacher rankings and fit, establish priorities for students in the "Priority" column. Record a "1" for the highest-priority student, and so on. Record an N/A for students who are deemed not to require intervention at this time.

(continued)

TASKS REQUIRING FOLLOW-UP

Student	Follow-Up Action	Who?	Date

Problem Identification Interview Form

Teacher(s): _____ Date: _____

School: _____

Interview Tasks

1. Select and rank-order target behaviors.
2. Operationally define each target behavior.
3. Establish procedures for baseline data collection.
4. Plan for next steps.
5. Schedule the DRC Design Interview.

1. Selection of Potential Target Behaviors

For the student of interest, identify three to five items from the screening form with the highest ratings and list them in the table.

Ranking	Problem Behaviors	DRC Item

(continued)

2. **Operationally Define Selected Target Behaviors**
   Use the Baseline Data Collection Form (Appendix D) to record operational definitions for each of the selected target behaviors. Make sure each definition is objective, clear, and complete.

3. **Establish Procedures for Baseline Data Collection**
   Make sure to specify the recording intervals (times of day when data will be recorded—by subject or by period or by time of day, e.g., A.M., P.M.). Once the data collection procedure is established, review it with teacher and ask him or her to repeat it back to ensure there is consensus on how the process will be enacted.

4. **Plan for Next Steps**

Check in on baseline data collection ("How is it going?")

Date: _____   Time: _____   Location: _____

DRC Design Interview

Date: _____   Time: _____   Location: _____

Establish how the teacher can reach you if there are questions regarding procedures.

DRC ITEM TABLE

Screening Items	DRC Items
1. Does not complete classwork on time	• Completes assignments within the allotted time • Stays on task with *X* or fewer reminders
2. Inaccurate or incomplete classwork	• Completes *X* assignments with *Y*% accuracy • Completes *X*% of assigned work
3. Does not start assignments independently	• Starts work with *X* or fewer reminders
4. Writes illegibly	• Leaves appropriate spaces between words *X*% of the time or assignment • Writes legibly/uses one-line cross-outs instead of scribbles/writes on the lines of the paper
5. Missing or incomplete homework	• Brings completed homework to class • Completes *X*% of assigned homework • Writes homework in assignment book with *X* or fewer reminders
6. Does not turn in class assignments	• Turns in assignments appropriately
7. Does not correct own work	• Corrects assignments appropriately
8. Fails to pack needed materials for home	• Has all needed materials for homework in backpack at the end of the day

(continued)

Screening Items	DRC Items
9. Transitions poorly between activities	• Walks in line appropriately • Lines up in timely fashion • Lines up in appropriate place • Lines up without touching other children • Follows transition rules with X or fewer violations • Changes into gym clothes/school clothes within X minutes
10. Argues with teacher	• No more than X arguments following feedback • Talks back fewer than X times
11. Disrespectful to adults	• Fewer than X instances of eye rolling or _____
12. Loses temper	• Asks for help when frustrated • Fewer than X temper outbursts
13. Does not ask for help/asks for help inappropriately	• Appropriately asks an adult for help when needed
14. Noncompliant	• Complies with $X\%$ of teacher commands/requests • Complies with teacher demand with fewer than X reminders
15. Disrupts others	• Interrupts class less than X times per period • Works quietly with X or fewer reminders • Makes X or fewer inappropriate noises • Fewer than X complaints from others • Fewer than X instances of talking when not appropriate
16. Does not follow directions	• Follow directions on work assignments
17. Calls out	• Raises hand to speak with X or fewer reminders
18. Moves around the room	• Sits appropriately in assigned area with X or fewer reminders
19. Uses materials inappropriately	• Uses materials or possessions appropriately
20. Uses inappropriate language	• Has fewer than X instances of cursing
21. Tattles on other children	• Has fewer than X instances of tattling on peers
22. Destroys property	• Has X or fewer instances of destroying property
23. Has conflicts with peers	• No physical fights with peers • Fewer than X instances of grabbing other's materials
24. Mumbles or speaks incoherently	• Fewer than X prompts for mumbling
25. Argues with peers	• Fewer than X arguments with peers
26. Bossy	• Needs X or fewer reminders to stop bossing peers
27. Nosey	• Minds own business with X or fewer reminders
28. Does not participate in group activities	• Shares/helps peers when appropriate with X or fewer reminders • Participates appropriately in group activities with fewer than X prompts

(continued)

Screening Items	DRC Items
29. Distracted by others' negative behaviors	• Ignores negative behavior of others/shows no observable response to negative behavior of others
30. Does not work well with others	• Shares/helps peers when appropriate with X or fewer reminders • Participates appropriately in group activities with fewer than X prompts
31. Teases	• Teases peers X or fewer times • Mocks or mimics others fewer than X times
32. Makes irrelevant comments	• At least X unprompted, relevant, nonredundant contributions
33. Comes to class unprepared	• Arrives to school/class with required materials
34. Unorganized	• Organizes material and possessions according to checklist/chart
35. Does not put away belongings	• Hangs up jacket/backpack with X or fewer reminders
36. Takes too long when using bathroom or water fountain	• Returns from water fountain or bathroom within X minutes
37. Asks to leave classroom frequently	• Asks to leave classroom fewer than X times
38. Makes self-deprecating comments	• Makes fewer than X negative self-statements
39. Cries, complains, whines	• Has X or fewer instances of crying/complaining/whining
40. Does not participate in class	• Appropriately contributes to class activities • Answers teacher questions • Answers peer questions
41. Leaves room without permission	• Leaves room only when appropriate
42. Bumps, hits, or kicks others	• Keeps hands and feet to self
43. Does not respect others' personal space	• Has fewer than X instances of invading others' space • Stays in own area with fewer than X reminders

Baseline Data Collection Form

Check-in for data collection will occur: Date/Day: _____ Time: _____

Teacher Name: _____ Data collected from _____ to _____

Student Name: _____

	Target Behavior 1	Target Behavior 2	Target Behavior 3	Target Behavior 4	Target Behavior 5	Target Behavior 6
Day 1						
Class/Period 1						
Class/Period 2						
Class/Period 3						
Class/Period 4						
Class/Period 5						
Day 2						
Class/Period 1						
Class/Period 2						
Class/Period 3						
Class/Period 4						
Class/Period 5						

Target Behaviors	Operational Definitions

(continued)

	Target Behavior 1	Target Behavior 2	Target Behavior 3	Target Behavior 4	Target Behavior 5	Target Behavior 6
Day 3						
Class/Period 1						
Class/Period 2						
Class/Period 3						
Class/Period 4						
Class/Period 5						
Day 4						
Class/Period 1						
Class/Period 2						
Class/Period 3						
Class/Period 4						
Class/Period 5						
Day 5						
Class/Period 1						
Class/Period 2						
Class/Period 3						
Class/Period 4						
Class/Period 5						

Notes

_____

_____

_____

_____

_____

_____

_____

Examples of DRCs

Daily Report Card

	Shared Reading	Writing	Read Aloud	Math	Science/Social Studies
1. Needs no more than one reminder to stay in assigned seat or area.	Y N	Y N	Y N	Y N	Y N
2. Needs no more than one reminder to work quietly (no shouting out/interrupting)	Y N	Y N	Y N	Y N	Y N
3. Assigned work is completed accurately and on time.	Y N	Y N	Y N	Y N	Y N
4. Returns completed homework with at least 80% accuracy	Y N N/A	Y N N/A	Y N N/A	Y N N/A	Y N N/A

Homework target percentage: _____ %

If homework percentage is greater than 80% for the week, the child can choose to have lunch in the classroom or have the teacher come to lunch!

OTHER

1. Reading class   +   ✓   –
2. Specials   +   ✓   –
3. Lunch   +   ✓   –

101

(continued)

Total Number of Yeses _____   Total Number of Nos _____   Percentage of Yeses _____

Comments: _____

_____

_____

_____

_____

_____

Parent: Please record reward provided _____

Parent: Please sign and return to teacher _____

(continued)

My Daily Report Card

Goal	Did I meet my goal?	
I hung up my jacket and backpack when I came in the classroom.	☺	☹
I finished my morning work on time.	☺	☹
I needed no more than two reminders to keep my hands to myself during the morning meeting on the rug.	☺	☹
I used my walking feet in the hallway.	☺	☹
I kept my hands to myself during lunch.	☺	☹
I needed no more than two reminders to stay in my area during quiet time.	☺	☹
I kept my hands and feet to myself in the bus line.	☺	☹

Comments: _____

Reward provided: _____

Parent signature: _____

(continued)

DRC Templates

SM-Daily Report Card   Student: _____   Date: _____

Behavior Goals   Period: _____   _____   _____   _____

1.   Y   N   Y   N   Y   N   Y   N

2.   Y   N   Y   N   Y   N   Y   N

3.   Y   N   Y   N   Y   N   Y   N

4.   Y   N   Y   N   Y   N   Y   N

Number of Yeses: _____ ÷ Number of Ratings: _____ = % or Goals Met: _____

(continued)

SM-Daily Report Card   Student: _____   Date: _____

Behavior Goals	Period:	____	____	____	____
1.		Y N	Y N	Y N	Y N
Examples:					
Non-examples:					
2.		Y N	Y N	Y N	Y N
Examples:					
Non-examples:					
3.		Y N	Y N	Y N	Y N
Examples:					
Non-examples:					
4.		Y N	Y N	Y N	Y N
Examples:					
Non-examples:					

Number of Yeses: _____ ÷ Number of Ratings: _____ = % or Goals Met: _____

(continued)

Daily Report Card   Student: _____   Date: _____

Behavior Goals   Period: _____   _____   _____   _____

1.   Y   N   Y   N   Y   N   Y   N

2.   Y   N   Y   N   Y   N   Y   N

3.   Y   N   Y   N   Y   N   Y   N

4.   Y   N   Y   N   Y   N   Y   N

Number of Yeses: _____ ÷ Number of Ratings: _____ = % or Goals Met: _____

Teacher Comments: _____

_____

_____

_____

_____

Home Rewards and Comments: _____

_____

_____

_____

_____

Teacher Initials: _____   Parent Initials: _____

Home Reward Planning Sheet

With your child, review these potential home rewards. As a first step, simply put a checkmark next to each reward your child indicates he or she would like to earn each day.

Home Privileges		
	_____	Minutes television time
	_____	Minutes computer time
	_____	Minutes video game time
	_____	Minutes extended bedtime
	_____	Minutes extended bathtime
	_____	Minutes phone time
	_____	Listen to radio/music at bedtime
	_____	Choose dinner
	_____	Choose dessert
	_____	Choose snack
	_____	Get out of a chore (specify: _____)
	_____	Special snack in tomorrow's lunch
	_____	Sleep in _____ minutes the next morning
	_____	Parent will drive to school the next morning
	_____	Daily cell phone privileges
	_____	Log-on privileges for social networking sites
	_____	Extra outdoor time past curfew
	_____	Use of bike
	_____	Use of scooter/skateboard/rollerblades
	_____	Have a friend over to play
Special Time with Parent	_____	Play a game with parent
	_____	Minutes one-on-one time
	_____	Drawing/coloring with parent
	_____	Reading a story with parent
	_____	Building with blocks
	_____	Playing video game together
	_____	Cooking with parent

(continued)

	_____	Watching home movies together
	_____	I spy/20 questions/knock-knock jokes with parent, etc.
	_____	Child-directed play activity with parents
	_____	Trip to the playground
	_____	Trip to the library
Tangibles	_____	Allowance/money
	_____	Gum
	_____	Candy
	_____	Stickers
	_____	Book
	_____	Toy
	_____	Videogame
	_____	Token that can contribute toward earning a toy/video game
	_____	Grab bag of toys/trinkets
	_____	Make a bid on eBay
	_____	Earn "coupons" for getting out of chores, trips to stores
	_____	Fast food
	_____	Go out for ice cream
	_____	Shopping for new clothes

DRC Contract and Parent Letter

The teacher will:

1. Provide positive encouragement for the attainment of goals throughout the day.
2. Rate each DRC item at the assigned time(s).
3. Make sure the DRC is sent home with the student.
4. Note any successes or problem areas that occurred.
5. Notify the parent via (phone, e-mail) if the DRC is not returned.

The parent will:

1. Review and sign the DRC and send it back to school to be returned to the teacher.
2. Provide rewards contingent on goal attainment daily and weekly.
3. Provide encouragement throughout the week for the attainment of daily and weekly goals.
4. Contact the teacher via (phone, e-mail, letter) if the DRC does not find its way home.

The student will:

1. Try his OR her very best to reach daily and weekly goals as outlined in the DRC.
2. Turn in the DRC with parent signature each school day.
3. Hand teacher-completed DRC to parent each school day.

Signatures

Teacher: _____

Parent: _____

Student: _____

(continued)

Dear [*Parent Name*]:

I have enjoyed working with [*child name*] so far this year. As you know, [*child name*] has been experiencing some challenges with [*list specific challenges here*] in class. It is my goal to keep working until I find an effective approach for every child in my class. In this case, I think it would be appropriate to try a Daily Report Card.

You might have had experience with something like this in the past. In my classroom the Daily Report Card represents a consistent approach by parents, the student, and me. I will help support [*child's name*] by providing clear and consistent feedback throughout the day. I am going to encourage [*child name*] to monitor his/her behavior and help him/her make the most out of each school day. I am going to ask you to support these efforts by providing positive consequences at home when [*child name*] is successful at meeting the Daily Report Card goals.

I would like to do this right, and I want to deal with the current challenges so that [*child name*] can be recognized for all the great skills and talents *he/she* has. Please let me know a time in the next week when we can talk or meet briefly to discuss next steps.

I am looking forward to speaking with you, and please be sure to let me know if you have any questions or concerns.

Best regards,

[*Teacher Name*]

[*Contact Information*]

DRC Design Interview Form

Teacher's name: _____   Child's name: _____

Observer's name: _____   Date: _____

DRC Interview Tasks

1. Review baseline data.
2. Establish goals for each item.
3. Establish setting and frequency of ratings.
4. Establish home reward system.
5. Establish procedures for progress monitoring.
6. Establish check-in schedule.
7. Establish goals for long-term success.
8. Schedule DRC Evaluation Interview.

1. Review baseline data (the interviewer should have a graph of baseline data to review with the teacher).
   a. Are there sufficient baseline data (i.e., at least 3–5 data points per target behavior; is baseline stable or does it indicate worsening)?

   b. Problem validation for each behavior: Is there indeed a problem? (Think about class/school norms for behavior in the settings observed.)

2. Establish goals for each item.
   a. What are the primary and/or most impairing presenting problems?

   b. Which behaviors, if targeted, might result in improvements in other behaviors?

3. Establish setting and frequency of ratings.
   a. Based on the answers to #2, above, when do these behaviors occur? (List all times and settings.)

_____

(continued)

4. How will the reward system work?
   a. Home- or school-based?

   b. Potential barriers to implementing the reward system?

   c. Concerns with adherence?

   d. What is rewarding to the child in school?

5. Establish procedures for progress monitoring.
   a. Who will chart data?

   b. How will data be transferred?

   c. Will accuracy be checked by consultant via observation?

6. Establish check-in schedule.
   a. At this point, who is responsible for particular aspects of the DRC intervention (monitoring progress, providing rewards, scheduling checkups)?

7. Establish goals for long-term success.
   a. What are the criteria for judging the DRC intervention as a success?

   b. What are the criteria for fading or withdrawing the intervention?

DRC Item	Settings	Goals	
		Short-term	Long-term

8. Schedule DRC Evaluation Interview.

   Date and time: _____

Treatment Integrity Form

Teacher's name: _____   Child's name: _____

Observer's name: _____   Date: _____

Use the checklist below to note the daily report card (DRC) procedures observed. It is recommended that the observation last 30 minutes or the duration of the class period evaluated on the DRC.

Check If Present	DRC Procedure
	Teacher reviewed DRC goals with the child prior to the evaluation period.
	Child was informed of violations or behaviors that occurred that were inconsistent with DRC goals.
	The teacher praised/attended to behaviors that were examples of positive behaviors/ consistent with meeting DRC goals.
	Feedback on DRC progress was provided in an ongoing fashion throughout the activity.
	Feedback was provided privately, if possible.
	Following the evaluation period, the teacher provided the child with feedback on meeting DRC goals.
	Feedback was provided using a positive tone for goals met and a neutral tone for goals that were not met.
	The child was reminded of the next opportunity to meet DRC goals.
	A review of returned DRCs indicates that parent(s) signed and provided a home-based reward, if applicable.
	School-based rewards are provided if home-based rewards are not applicable.

Use the checkboxes below to mark the teacher's consistency in evaluating DRC targets.

Write the DRC targets below.	Child exhibited the targeted behavior.	Teacher provided feedback regarding the targeted behavior.

_____/_____ = _____

Teacher feedback   /Total exhibited   = % targeted behaviors accurately recorded

(continued)

Rate the quality of implementation of the DRC intervention.

1. The teacher used the DRC as intended, based on the intervention plan.

1 Did not use appropriately at all	2	3	4	5	6	7 Used appropriately

2. The teacher used an appropriate tone when providing feedback on DRC goals.

1 Not appropriate at all	2	3	4	5	6	7 Very appropriate

3. The teacher was consistent in implementing the DRC, based on the intervention plan.

1 Did not use consistently at all	2	3	4	5	6	7 Used very consistently

4. Please rate the overall effectiveness of the DRC intervention used.

1 Did not use effectively at all	2	3	4	5	6	7 Used very effectively

DRC Evaluation Interview Form

Teacher(s): _____ Date: _____

School: _____

Interview Tasks

1. Determine the extent to which goals of the DRC intervention have been met.
2. Determine if changes are needed (discontinue, revise, persist).
3. Plan for next steps.

Items Needed for Interview

1. Charted single-case design data for each DRC item and for total problems.
2. Notes from DRC Design Interview.
3. Permanent products and notes pertaining to treatment integrity.

1. Goal Attainment

Have the long-term goals for each DRC target been met?

DRC Item	Long-Term Goal	Goal Met? (Y, N)	If No, Adequate Progress? (Y, N)

(continued)

2. **What, if any, changes are needed to the program?**

3. **Next Steps**

Follow-Up Action	Who?	Date

SM-DRC Training Form

Teacher(s): _____   Date: _____

School: _____

Training Tasks

1. Review items and ensure that language is student-friendly.
2. Brainstorm examples and non-examples of target behavior(s).
3. Demonstrate and practice rating procedures.
4. Discuss the rationale for self-monitoring component.
5. Establish procedures for data collection.

1. **Review items and ensure that language is student-friendly.**
   Although items should be directly transferred from the DRC, modifications may be needed to make the language more easily understandable to the student. For example, "Raise hand when I need help" may be easier for students to assess than "Appropriately asks an adult for help when needed."

Original DRC Item	Modified SM-DRC Item

(continued)

2. **Brainstorm examples and non-examples of target behaviors.**
   Help the student to identify both examples and non-examples of the target behavior that can be listed on the SM-DRC.

Target behavior	Examples	Non-examples

3. **Demonstrate and practice rating procedures.**
   Provide the student with the actual SM-DRC and ask him/her to rate the items as examples or non-examples as the target behaviors are acted out.

4. **Discuss the rationale for self-monitoring component.**
   Discuss with the student the reason for transitioning from teacher to self-ratings (e.g., take control of own behavior).

5. **Establish procedures for data collection.**
   Make sure to specify the recording intervals (times of day when data will be recorded—by subject/period or by time of day, e.g., A.M., P.M.). Once data collection procedure is established, review the procedure with student and ask him or her to repeat it back to check for understanding.

Additional Resources

Additional resources are available (some for free) for educators interested in using DRCs in schools. Although reviewing all available resources is outside the scope of this book, we list some helpful ones to illustrate the availability of additional material on this topic. Below are examples of some resources that may be helpful in addition to this book.

INTERNET RESOURCES

How to Establish a Daily Report Card (School–Home Note; Pelham, 2012)

http://casgroup.fiu.edu/pages/docs/1401/1321381613_How_To_Establish_a_School_DRC.pdf

This 10-page handout is a straightforward and useful guide for constructing a DRC from start to finish. Created by one of the developers of the DRC for use with children with ADHD, William E. Pelham, Jr., this online guide is free of charge and easy to use. The blank handouts and supporting materials include everything an educator would need to establish targets and goal criteria and create reward menus for school and/or home; there is a troubleshooting page that helps support the maintenance of the DRC in an ongoing fashion.

Behavior Report Card Maker (Wright, 2012)

www.interventioncentral.org/tools/behavior-report-card-maker

Using an online series of prompts, Jim Wright has created a way for educators to select targets, format the DRC, and set up evaluation periods for each goal (e.g., by time of day) in a very user-friendly way. Once the educator enters the appropriate information, the program will create a .pdf document that can be printed and implemented with the targeted child.

Psychological Software Solutions

www.psiwaresolutions.com

This company offers a host of web-based products for the implementation of schoolwide, classwide, and individual behavioral supports. Tools include universal screening, professional development, online training for empirically supported interventions, incident tracking, and a web-based system for the implementation of DRC.

Electronic Daily Behavior Report Card System (e-DBRC; Vannest, Burke, & Adiguzel, 2006)

http://e-dbrc.tamu.edu

A web-based electronic DRC program. At the time of this writing the system is offered free of charge. There are several resources on the site, including a downloadable manual and training guide. Also available are several preformatted DRC forms in a variety of formats.

Evidence-Based Intervention Network—Behavioral Contracts (Riley-Tillman, 2012)

http://ebi.missouri.edu/wp-content/uploads/2011/09/Behavior-Contracts.pdf

The behavioral contract handout on the EBI Network outlines procedures that can be used to implement a DRC in a contract format. This format may be especially helpful for older children in middle or high school when they are more capable of keeping track of goals throughout the school day, and when target behaviors may occur less frequently than in younger children.

BOOKS

Crone, D. A., & Horner, R. H. (2003). *Building positive behavior support systems in schools: Functional behavioral assessment*. New York: Guilford Press.

DuPaul, G. J., & Stoner, G. (2003). *ADHD in the schools: Assessment and intervention strategies* (2nd ed.). New York: Guilford Press.

Kelly, M. L. (1990). *School–home notes: Promoting Children's Classroom Success*. New York: Guilford Press.

Riley-Tillman, T. C., & Burns, M. K. (2009). *Evaluating educational interventions: Single-case design for measuring response to intervention*. New York: Guilford Press.

Sheridan, S. M., & Kratochwill, T. R. (2007). *Conjoint behavioral consultation: Promoting family–school connections and interventions*. New York: Springer.

References

American Psychological Association. (2006). Report on the teacher needs survey. Retrieved from *www. apa.org/ed/schools/coalition/teachers-needs.pdf*.

Baer, D. M., Wolf, M. M., & Risley, T. R. (1968). Some current dimensions of applied behavior analysis. *Journal of Applied Behavior Analysis, 1*, 91–97.

Bailey, J. S., Wolf, M. M., & Phillips, E. L. (1970). Home-based reinforcement and the modification of pre-delinquents' classroom behavior. *Journal of Applied Behavior Analysis, 3*, 223–233.

Barkley, R. A. (1997). *Defiant children: A clinician's manual for assessment and parent training* (2nd ed.). New York: Guilford Press.

Bergan, J. (1977). *Behavioral consultation*. Columbus, OH: Merrell.

Blechman, E. A., Taylor, C. J., & Schrader, S. M. (1981). Family problem-solving versus home notes as early intervention with high risk children. *Journal of Consulting and Clinical Psychology, 6*, 919–926.

Briesch, A., & Volpe, R. J. (2007). Selecting progress monitoring tools for evaluating social behavior. *School Psychology Forum, 1*, 59–74.

Brown, R. T., Antonuccio, D. O., DuPaul, G. J., Fristad, M. A., King, C. A., Leslie, L. K., et al. (2008). *Childhood mental health disorders*. Washington, DC: American Psychological Association.

Burke, M. D., Vannest, K., Davis, J., Davis, C., & Parker, R. (2009). Reliability of frequent retrospective behavior ratings for elementary school students with EBD. *Behavioral Disorders, 34*, 212–222.

Caldarella, P., Young, E. L., Richardson, M. J., Young, B. J., & Young, K. R. (2008). Validation of the Systematic Screening for Behavioral Disorders in middle and junior high school. *Journal of Emotional and Behavioral Disorders, 16*, 105–117.

Cartwright, C. A., & Cartwright, G. P. (1970). Determining the motivational systems of individual children. *Teaching Exceptional Children, 2*, 143–149.

Chafouleas, S. M. (2011). Direct behavior rating: A review of the issues and research in its development. *Education and Treatment of Children, 34*, 575–591.

Chafouleas, S. M., Briesch, A. M., Riley-Tillman, T. C., Christ, T. C., Black, A. C., & Kilgus, S. P. (2010). An investigation of the generalizability and dependability of Direct Behavior Rating Single Item Scales (DBR-SIS) to measure academic engagement and disruptive behavior of middle school students. *Journal of School Psychology, 48*, 219–246.

Chafouleas, S. M., Christ, T. J., & Riley-Tillman, T. C. (2009). Generalizability of scaling gradients on Direct Behavior Ratings (DBRs). *Educational and Psychological Measurement, 69*, 157-173.

Chafouleas, S. M., Christ, T. J., Riley-Tillman, T. C., Briesch, A. M., & Chanese, J. A. M. (2007). Generalizability and dependability of direct behavior ratings to assess social behavior of preschoolers. *School Psychology Review, 36*, 63–79.

Chafouleas, S. M., Riley-Tillman, T. C., & Sassu, K. A. (2006). Acceptability and reported use of daily behavior report cards among teachers. *Journal of Positive Behavior Interventions, 8*, 174–182.

Chafouleas, S. M., Riley-Tillman, T. C., Sassu, K. A., LaFrance, M. J., & Patwa, S. S. (2007). The consistency of daily behavior report cards in monitoring interventions. *Journal of Positive Behavior Interventions, 9*, 30–37.

Chafouleas, S. M., Sanetti, L. M. H., Kilgus, S. P., & Maggin, D. M. (2013). Evaluating sensitivity to behavioral change across consultation cases using direct behavior rating single-item scales (DBR-SIS). *Exceptional Children, 78*, 491–505.

Chafouleas, S. M., Volpe, R. J., Gresham, F. M., & Cook, C. R. (2010). Behavioral assessment within problem-solving models: Current status and future directions. *School Psychology Review, 39*, 343–349.

Christ, T. J., & Boice, C. (2009). Rating scale items: A brief review of nomenclature, components, and formatting to inform the development of direct behavior rating (DBR). *Assessment for Effective Intervention, 34*, 242–250.

Christ, T. J., Riley-Tillman, T. C., Chafouleas, S., & Jaffery, R. (2011). Direct behavior rating: An evaluation of alternate definitions to assess classroom behaviors. *School Psychology Review, 40*, 181–199.

Coalition for Psychology in the Schools and Education. (2006, August). Report on the Teacher Needs Survey. Washington, DC: American Psychological Association, Center for Psychology in Schools and Education.

Conduct Problems Prevention Research Group. (1999). Initial Impact of the Fast Track Prevention Trial for Conduct Problems: I. The High-Risk Sample. *Journal of Consulting and Clinical Psychology, 67*(5), 631–647.

Cook, C., Gresham, F. M., & Volpe, R. J. (2012). *Manual for the Student Internalizing and Externalizing Behavior Screeners*. Houston, TX: Psychological Software Solutions.

Cook, C., Volpe, R. J., & Livanis, A. (2010). Constructing a roadmap for future universal screening research beyond academics. *Assessment for Effective Intervention, 35*, 197–205.

Cooper, J. O., Heron, T. E., & Heward, W. L. (2007). *Applied behavior analysis* (2nd ed.). Upper Saddle River, NJ: Pearson Education.

DiPerna, J. C., Volpe, R. J., & Elliott, S. N. (2001). A model of academic enablers and academic achievement. *School Psychology Review, 31*, 298–312.

DiPerna, J. C., Volpe, R. J., & Elliott, S. N. (2005). An examination of academic enablers and achievement in mathematics. *Journal of School Psychology, 43*, 379–392.

Dougherty, E. H., & Dougherty, A. (1977). The daily behavior report card: A simplified and flexible package for classroom behavior management. *Psychology in the Schools, 14*, 191–195.

Dussault, W. L. E. (1996). Avoiding due process hearings: Developing an open relationship between parents and school districts. In L. K. Koegel, R. L. Koegel, & G. Dunlap (Eds.), *Positive behavioral support: Including people with difficult behavior in the community* (pp. 265–278). Baltimore, MD: Brookes.

Elliott, S. N., & Gresham, F. M. (2007). *Social Skills Improvement System: Performance screening guides*. Bloomington, MN: Pearson Assessments.

Evans, S. W., & Youngstrom, E. (2006). Evidence-based assessment of attention-deficit/hyperactivity disorder: Measuring outcomes. *Journal of the American Academy of Child and Adolescent Psychiatry, 45*, 1132–1137.

Fabiano, G. A., Pelham, W. E., Gnagy, E. M., Burrows-MacLean, L., Coles, E. K., Chacko, A., et al. (2007). The single and combined effects of multiple intensities of behavior modification and multiple intensities of methylphenidate in a classroom setting. *School Psychology Review, 36,* 195–216.

Fabiano, G. A., Vujnovic, R., Naylor, J., Pariseau, M., & Robins, M. (2009a). An investigation of the technical adequacy of a daily behavior report card (DBRC) for monitoring progress of students with attention-deficit/hyperactivity disorder in special education placements. *Assessment for Effective Intervention, 34,* 231–241.

Fabiano, G. A., Pelham, W. E., Coles, E. K., Gnagy, E. M., Chronis, A. M., & O'Connor, B. (2009b). A meta-analysis of behavioral treatments for attention-deficit/hyperactivity disorder. *Clincial Psychology Review, 29*(2), 129–140.

Fabiano, G. A., Vujnovic, R., Pelham, W. E., Waschbusch, D. A., Massetti, G. M., Yu, J., et al. (2010). Enhancing the effectiveness of special education programming for children with ADHD using a daily report card. *School Psychology Review, 39,* 219–239.

Fuchs, D., & Fuchs, L. S. (1989). Exploring effective and efficient pre-referral interventions: A component analysis of behavioral consultation. *School Psychology Review, 18,* 260–283.

Gable, R. A., & Shores, R. E. (1980). Comparison of procedures for promoting reading proficiency of two children with behavioral and learning disorders. *Behavioral Disorders, 5,* 102–107.

Glover, T. A., & Albers, C. A. (2007). Considerations for evaluating universal screening assessments. *Journal of School Psychology. 45,* 117–135.

Gresham, F. M. (2005). Response to intervention: An alternative means of identifying students as emotionally disturbed. *Education and Treatment of Children. 28.* 328–344.

Gunter, P. L., Denny, R. I. C., Jack, S. U., Shores, R. E., & Nelson, C. M. (1993). Aversive stimuli in academic interactions between students with serious emotional disturbance and their teachers. *Behavioral Disorders, 18,* 265–274.

Hamre, B. K., & Pianta, R. C. (2001). Early teacher–child relationships and the trajectory of children's school outcomes through eighth grade. *Child Development, 72,* 625–638.

Hinshaw, S. P. (1992). Academic underachievement, attention deficits, and aggression: Comorbidity and implications for interventions. *Journal of Consulting and Clinical Psychology, 60,* 893–903.

Horner, R. H., Sugai, G., Todd, A. W., & Lewis-Palmer, T. (2000). Elements of behavior support plans: A technical brief. *Exceptionality, 8,* 205–216.

Hughes, J. N., Cavell, T. A., & Wilson, V. (2001). Further support for the developmental significance of the quality of the teacher–student relationship. *Journal of School Psychology, 39,* 289–302.

Johnson, J. M., & Pennypacker, H. S. (1993). *Readings for strategies and tactics of behavioral research* (2nd ed.). Hillsdale, NJ: Erlbaum.

Kalberg, J. R., Lane, K. L., Driscoll, S., & Wehby, J. (2011). Systematic screening for emotional and behavior disorders at the high school level: A formidable and necessary task. *Remedial and Special Education, 32,* 506–520.

Kamphaus, R. W., DiStefano, C., Dowdy, E., Eklund, K., & Dunn, A. R. (2010). Determining the presence of a problem: Comparing two approaches for detecting youth behavioral risk. *School Psychology Review, 39,* 395–407.

Kamphaus, R. W., & Reynolds, C. R. (2007). *BASC-2 Behavioral and Emotional Screening System.* Minneapolis, MN: Pearson Assessment.

Kanfer, F. H. (1970). Self-monitoring: Methodological considerations and clinical applications. *Journal of Consulting and Clinical Psychology, 35,* 148–152.

Kauffman, J. M., Mock, D. R., & Simpson, R. L. (2007). Problems related to under-service of students with emotional or behavioral disorders. *Behavioral Disorders, 33,* 43–57.

Kazdin, A. E. (2010). *Single-case research designs: Methods for clinical and applied settings* (2nd ed.). New York: Oxford University Press.

Kelley, M. L. (1990). School–home notes: Promoting children's classroom success. New York: Guilford Press.

Koegel, L. K., & Koegel, R. L. (1996). Discussion: Education issues. In L. K. Koegel, R. L. Koegel, & G. Dunlap (Eds.), *Positive behavioral support: Including people with difficult behavior in the community* (pp. 265–278). Baltimore, MD: Brookes Publishing.

Kratochwill, T. R., & Bergan, J. R. (1990). *Behavioral consultation in applied settings: An individual guide.* New York: Plenum Press.

Ladd, G. W., & Burgess, K. B. (2001). Do relational risks and protective factors moderate the linkages between childhood aggression and early psychological and school adjustment? *Child Development, 72,* 1579–1601.

Lahey, B. B., Gendrich, J. G., Gendrich, S. I., Schnelle, J. F., Gant, D. S., & McNees, M. P. (1977). An evaluation of daily behavior report cards with minimal teacher and parent contacts as an efficient method of classroom intervention. *Behavior Modification, 1,* 381–394.

Lane, K. L., Menzies, H. M., Oakes, W. P., & Kalberg, J. R. (2012). *Systematic screenings of behavior to support instruction: From preschool to highschool.* New York: Guilford Press.

Lane, K. L., Wehby, J., Robertson, E. J., & Rogers, L. (2007). How do different types of high school students respond to positive behavior support programs?: Characteristics and responsiveness of teacher-identified students. *Journal of Emotional and Behavioral Disorders, 15,* 3–20.

Loney, J., & Milich, R. (1982). Hyperactivity, inattention, and aggression in clinical practice. In M. Wolraich & D. K. Routh (Eds.), *Advances in developmental and behavioral pediatrics* (Vol. 3, pp. 113–147). Greenwich, CT: JAI Press.

Martens, B. K., & Ardoin, S. P. (2002). Training school psychologists in behavior support consultation. *Child and Family Behavior Therapy, 24,* 147–163.

McCain, A., & Kelley, M. L. (1994). Improving classroom performance in underachieving preadolescents: The additive effects of response cost to a school–home note system. *Child and Family Behavior Therapy, 16,* 27–41.

McGoey, K. E., & DuPaul, G. J. (2000). Token reinforcement and response cost procedures: Reducing the disruptive behavior of preschool children. *School Psychology Quarterly, 15,* 330–343.

McIntosh, K., Frank, J., & Spaulding, S. A. (2010). Establishing research-based trajectories of office discipline referrals for individual students. *School Psychology Review, 39,* 380–394.

McIntosh, K., Goodman, S., & Bohanon, H. (2010). Toward true integration of academic and behavioral response to intervention systems: Part One. Tier 1 support. *NASP Communiqué, 38,* 1; 14–25.

McKinney, E., Bartholomew, C., & Gray, L. (2010). RTI and SWPBIS: Confronting the problem of disproportionality. *NASP Communiqué, 38,* 6.

Moore, L. A., Waguespack, A. M., Wickstrom, K. F., Witt, J. C., & Gaydon, G. R. (1994). Mystery motivator: An effective and time efficient intervention. *School Psychology Review, 23,* 106–117.

MTA Cooperative Group. (1999). 14-month randomized clinical trial of treatment strategies for attention deficit hypeactivity disorder. *Archives of General Psychiatry, 56,* 1073–1086.

O'Leary, K. D., Pelham, W. E., Rosenbaum, A., & Price, G. H. (1976). Behavioral treatment of hyperkinetic children. *Clinical Pediatrics, 15,* 510–515.

O'Leary, S. G., & Pelham, W. E. (1978). Behavior therapy and withdrawal of stimulant medication in hyperactive children. *Pediatrics, 61,* 211–217.

Ollendick, T. H., Greene, R. W., Weist, M. D., & Oswald, D. P. (1990). The predictive validity of teacher nominations: A five-year follow up of at-risk youth. *Journal of Abnormal Child Psychology, 18,* 699–713.

Pelham, W. E. (1993). Pharmacotherapy for children with attention-deficit/hyperactivity disorder. *School Psychology Review, 21,* 199–223.

Pelham, W. E., & Fabiano, G. A. (2008). Evidence-based psychosocial treatment for ADHD: An update. *Journal of Clinical Child and Adolescent Psychology, 37,* 184–214.

Pelham, W. E., Fabiano, G. A., & Massetti, G. M. (2005). Evidence-based assessment for attention-deficit/hyperactivity disorder in children and adolescents. *Journal of Clinical Child and Adolescent Psychology, 34,* 449–476.

Pelham, W. E., Gnagy, E. M., Burrows-Maclean, L., Williams, A., Fabiano, G. A., Morrissey, S. M., et al. (2001). Once-a-day Concerta methylphenidate versus three-times-daily methylphenidate in laboratory and natural settings. *Pediatrics, 107*(6), e105. Retrieved January 7, 2009, from *www.pediatrics.org/cgi/content/full/107/6/e105.*

Pelham, W. E., Hoza, B., Pillow, D. R., Gnagy, E. M., Kipp, H. L., Greiner, A. R., et al. (2002). Effects of methylphenidate and expectancy on children with ADHD: Behavior, academic performance, and attributions in a summer treatment program and regular classroom settings. *Journal of Consulting and Clinical Psychology, 70,* 320–335.

Pelham, W. E., Massetti, G. M., Wilson, T., Kipp, H., Myers, D., Newman, B. B., et al. (2005). Implementation of a comprehensive school-wide behavioral intervention: The ABC program. *Journal of Attention Deficit Disorders, 9,* 248–260.

Pianta, R. C., Steinberg, M. S., & Rollins, K. B. (1995). The first two years of school: Teacher–child relationships and deflections in children's classroom adjustment. *Development and Psychopathology, 7,* 295–312.

Premack, D. (1959). Toward empirical behavioral laws: I. Positive reinforcement. *Psychological Review, 66,* 219-233.

Public Agenda. (2004). Teaching interrupted: Do discipline policies in today's public schools foster the common good? Retrieved from *www.publicagenda.org/files/pdf/teaching_interrupted.pdf.*

Rhode, G., Jenson, W. R., & Reavis, H. K. (1992). *The tough kid book.* Longmont, CO: Sopris West.

Riley-Tillman, T. C., & Burns, M. K. (2009). *Evaluating educational interventions: Single-case design for measuring response to intervention.* New York: Guilford Press.

Riley-Tillman, T. C., Chafouleas, S. M., & Briesch, A. M. (2007). A school practitioner's guide to using daily behavior report cards to monitor student behavior. *Psychology in the Schools, 44,* 77–89.

Riley-Tillman, T. C., Chafouleas, S. M., Briesch, A. M., & Eckert, T. L. (2008). Daily behavior report cards and systematic direct observation: An investigation of the acceptability, reported training and use, and decision reliability among school psychologists. *Journal of Behavioral Education, 17,* 313–327.

Riley-Tillman, T. C., Chafouleas, S. M., Christ, T. C., Briesch, A. M., & LeBel, T. J. (2009). The impact of item wording and behavioral specificity on the accuracy of Direct Behavior Ratings (DBRs). *School Psychology Quarterly, 24,* 1–12.

Riley-Tillman, T. C., Christ, T. J., Chafouleas, S. M., Boice-Mallach, C. H., & Briesch, A. M. (2011). The impact of observation duration on the accuracy of data obtained from direct behavior rating (DBR). *Journal of Positive Behavior Interventions, 13,* 119–128.

Romer, D., & McIntosh, M. (2005). The roles and perspectives of school mental health professionals in promoting adolescent mental health. In D. L. Evans, E. B. Foa, R. E. Gur, H. Hendin, C. P. O'Brien, M. E. P. Seligman, et al. (Eds.), *Treating and preventing adolescent health disorders: What we know and what we don't know* (pp. 598–615). New York: Oxford University Press.

Saudargas, R. A., Madsen, C. H., & Scott, J. W. (1977). Differential effects of fixed- and variable-time feedback on production rates of elementary school children. *Journal of Applied Behavior Analysis, 10,* 673–678.

Schlientz, M. D., Riley-Tillman, T. C., Briesch, A. M., Walcott, C. M., & Chafouleas, S. M. (2009). The impact of training on the accuracy of direct behavior ratings (DBRs). *School Psychology Quarterly, 24,* 73–83.

Schumaker, J. B., Hovell, M. F., & Sherman, J. A. (1977). An analysis of daily behavior report cards and parent-managed privileges in the improvement of adolescents' classroom performance. *Journal of Applied Behavior Analysis, 10,* 449–464.

Severson, H. H., Walker, H. M., Hope-Doolittle, J., Kratochwill, T. R., & Gresham, F. M. (2007). Proactive, early screening to detect behaviorally at-risk students: Issues, approaches, emerging innovations, and professional practices. *Journal of School Psychology, 45,* 193–223.

Shores, R. E., Jack, S. L., Gunter, P. L., Ellis, D. N., DeBriere, T. J., & Wehby, J. H. (1993). Classroom interactions of children with behavior disorders. *Journal of Emotional and Behavioral Disorders, 1,* 27–39.

Sidman, M. (1960). *Tactics of scientific research.* New York: Basic Books.

Sugai, G., & Colvin, G. (1997). Debriefing: A transition step for promoting acceptable behavior. *Education and Treatment of Children, 20,* 209–221.

Sutherland, K. S., Wehby, J. H., & Copeland, S. R. (2000). Effect of varying rates of behavior-specific praise on the on-task behavior of students with EBD. *Journal of Emotional and Behavioral Disorders, 8,* 2–8.

U.S. Department of Education, Institute of Education Sciences, What Works Clearinghouse. (2006). *Check and connect.* Washington, DC: Author.

U.S. Department of Education, Office of Special Education and Rehabilitative Services, Office of Special Education Programs. (2004). *Teaching children with attention-deficit/hyperactivity disorder: Instructional strategies and practices.* Washington, DC: Author.

Vannest, K., Burke, M., & Adiguzel, T. (2006). *Electronic daily behavior report card (e-DBRC): A web-based system for progress monitoring* (Beta version) [Web-based application]. College Station: Texas A&M University. Retrieved June 28, 2012, from *http://e-dbrc.tamu.edu.*

Vannest, K. J., Burke, M. D., Parker, R., Davis, J., Barrios, L., & Davis, C. (in press). Technical adequacy, reliability and applications of DBRC progress monitoring measures with secondary students and severe problem behavior. *Remedial and Special Education.*

Vannest, K. J., Burke, M. D., Payne, T. E., Davis, C. R., & Soars, D. A. (2011). Electronic progress monitoring of IEP goals and objectives. *Teaching Exceptional Children, 43,* 40–51.

Vannest, K. J., Davis, J. L., Davis, C. R., Mason, B. A., & Burke, M. D. (2010). Effective intervention and measurement with a daily behavior report card: A meta-analysis. *School Psychology Review, 39,* 654–672.

Volkow, N. D., & Swanson, J. M. (2008). Does childhood treatment of ADHD with stimulant medication affect substance abuse in adulthood? *American Journal of Psychiatry, 65,* 553–555.

Volpe, R. J., Briesch, A. M., & Chafouleas, S. M. (2010). Linking screening for emotional and behavioral problems to problem-solving efforts: An adaptive model of behavioral assessment. *Assessment for Effective Intervention, 35,* 240–244.

Volpe, R. J., Briesch, A. M., & Gadow, K. D. (2011). The efficiency of behavior rating scales to assess disruptive classroom behavior: Applying generalizability theory to streamline assessment. *Journal of School Psychology, 49,* 131–155.

Volpe, R. J., DuPaul, G. J., DiPerna, J. C., Jitendra, A. K., Lutz, J. G., Tresco, K., et al. (2006). Attention-deficit/hyperactivity disorder and scholastic achievement: Models of mediation via academic enablers. *School Psychology Review, 35,* 47–61.

Volpe, R. J., Fabiano, G. A., & Briesch, A. M. (2012). *The Integrated Screening and Intervention System: Linking universal screening to intervention design.* Manuscript in preparation.

Volpe, R. J., & Gadow, K. D. (2010). Creating abbreviated rating scales to monitor classroom inattention–overactivity, aggression, and peer conflict: Reliability, validity, and treatment sensitivity. *School Psychology Review, 39,* 350–363.

Walker, H. M., & Hops, H. (1979). The CLASS program for acting out children: R&D procedures, program outcomes and implementation issues. *School Psychology Review, 8,* 370–381.

Walker, H. M., Retana, G. F., & Gersten, R. (1988). Replication of the CLASS program in Costa Rica: Implementation procedures and program outcomes. *Behavior Modification, 12,* 133–154.

Walker, H. M., & Severson, H. H. (1990). *Systematic screening for behavior disorders (SSBD)*. Longmont, CO: Sopris West.

Wehby, J. H., Symons, F. J., & Shores, R. E. (1995). A descriptive analysis of aggressive behavior in classrooms for children with emotional and behavioral disorders. *Behavioral Disorders, 20*, 87–105.

Witt, J. C., & Elliott, S. N. (1985). Acceptability of classroom management strategies. In T. R. Kratochwill (Ed.), *Advances in school psychology* (Vol. 4, pp. 251–288). Hillsdale, NJ: Erlbaum.

Witt, J. C., Martens, B. K., & Elliott, S. N. (1984). Factors affecting teachers' judgments of the acceptability of behavioral interventions: Time involvement, behavior problem severity, type of intervention. *Behavior Therapy, 15*, 204–209.

Index